The Language of
Advertising and Merchandising
in English

English
for
Careers

The Language of Advertising and Merchandising in English

David P. Rein

Regents Publishing Company, Inc.

Cover: photo courtesy
  Vango Media, Inc.
Cover design by
  Suzanne Bennett
Text design by
  Grace Kao
Photo Research by
  Monique Peyrat

10 9 8 7 6 5 4 3

Published by
Regents Publishing Company,
Inc.
2 Park Avenue
New York, N.Y. 10016

Printed in the United States of
America
ISBN 0-88345-353-3

Table of Contents

Photo Credits:

Foreword

This book is one of a series called *English for Careers.* The books in the series introduce students to careers in which English is widely used throughout the world. The books are intended for high intermediate or advanced learners who already know the basic structures of English. Students will benefit from these books in two major ways. They will learn the technical vocabulary of their specific field of interest. They will also improve their overall ability to communicate in English.

The Language of Advertising and Merchandising in English consists of ten units. Each unit begins with definitions of technical terms. These are followed by practice of the new vocabulary in context. All of these words and expressions appear in the reading, which fully investigates and explains a significant aspect of advertising and merchandising. Next, a review exercise tests students' comprehension of what they have read. Discussion questions give students opportunities to talk about their profession in English, and to apply new knowledge directly and immediately.

The first nine units of this book follow the format of an advertising campaign. The plan begins with the results of research of the market, the consumer, and the product. (Units 1-3). Unit 4 tells how the product's price, package and brand name communicate the product concept to consumers. Unit 5 lists the objectives and strategies for selling the product. Units 6-8 tell which media will be used, how, and to what extent. Finally, Unit 9 gives objectives and strategies for merchandising a product. Unit 10 is about careers in the field of advertising and merchandising.

Advertising and merchandising are part of the marketing process, the most visible to consumers. To the average person, "advertising" is any effort that helps to sell the product. In the vocabulary of marketing, that is "promotion." "Advertising" has a more precise meaning: paid promotion in the major media. Both definitions are used here. Merchandising supplements advertising. It takes two forms, sales promotion and promotion in minor media. Advertising prepares potential consumers to buy a product. Merchandising moves them toward actual purchase.

This book concentrates on national advertising of consumer goods. However, the principles discussed generally apply to other forms of advertising and to other kinds of products as well. The purpose of all advertising and merchandising is to communicate, inform and persuade.

David P. Rein
Hartford, Connecticut

The Market

Special Terms

Marketing
>   All activities that move goods from producers to consumers: production, promotion, distribution, packaging, pricing.

Consumer
>   One member of the market; the user of a product.

Market
>   People who can and will make purchases to satisfy their needs.

Product
>   In marketing, a consumer good, an industrial good, a service, or an idea.
>   One specific product in a category; a brand.

Marketing concept
>   The idea, basic to modern marketing, that goods are produced in response to consumers' needs.

Advertising
>   Promotion; any means of promoting the sale and use of a product.
>   In marketing, paid promotion through the major media.

Merchandising
>   Sales promotion; paid promotion through minor media.

Secondary data
>   Information used in a specific research project but gathered originally for a different purpose.

Primary data
>   Information gathered for the first time for a specific research project.

Qualitative research
>   Exploratory or subjective research. Its purpose is to obtain general feelings and impressions.

Quantitative research
>Conclusive or objective research. Its purpose is to reach definite conclusions.

MIS
>Marketing Information System. A computer-based system for analyzing data for use in making marketing decisions.

Market share
>One producer's percentage of the market for a product category; brand share.

Distribution
>Moving goods from one place to another before their sale to consumers, for example, from producer to wholesaler; from wholesaler to retailer.

BDI
>Brand-development index. It compares sales of a brand to total sales in the product category.

CDI
>Category-development index. It compares sales in the product category to sales in the geographical region.

Store-count distribution
>The number of stores that carry a given brand.

ACV
>All-commodity volume. It represents the total amount of sales in a product category.

Vocabulary Practice

1. What is the difference between a *market* and a *consumer?*

2. Give two definitions of a *product.*

3. Give a general definition of *advertising.*

4. Give a specific definition of advertising, as used in marketing.

5. Name two forms of *merchandising.*

6. Name five aspects of *marketing.*

7. What is the *marketing concept?*

8. What is the difference between *secondary data* and *primary data?*

9. What is the difference between *qualitative research* and *quantitative research?*

10. What does *MIS* stand for? Describe MIS and its use.

11. Define *market share.* Give a synonym for it.

12. Give an example of *distribution.*

13. What does *BDI* stand for? Which sales figures does it compare?

14. What does *CDI* stand for? Which sales figures does it compare?

15. Define *store-count distribution.*

16. What does *ACV* stand for? Define it.

The Market

Communicating the marketing concept

Marketing begins with a consumer need. Something is produced in response to that need. In a marketing society, the *consumer* rules. Marketing societies have produced a great abundance and variety of consumer goods. They have done this by means of competition. Each producer competes with every other producer for a share of the *market.* The market, simply, is people who have money and are ready to spend it. But consumers have a finite amount of money to spend. They will buy only what they want and need. As a nation becomes more developed, consumers become more demanding. Their needs become more specific, and they want *products* that satisfy their changing needs. Only those producers who compete effectively will sell their products and survive.

Successful producers are guided by the *marketing concept:* response to consumers' needs.

Marketing is a matter of communication between consumers and producers. *Advertising* is not the producer's only means of communication. The product itself, its packaging, brand name, and price carry a message to the potential user. So does the place where the product is sold. Marketing communications, then, can be defined as all marketing activities visible to consumers that may influence their purchasing decisions. These activities include both advertising and *merchandising.* Everyone involved in those activities is a marketing communicator. The basis of all marketing communication is one essential question: "How can we best inform consumers that our product meets their needs?" The answer to that question is what an advertising campaign is all about.

Market research

Planning an advertising campaign begins with an analysis of the market situation. Situation analysis moves from the general to the specific. It begins with the broad economic picture. Is this a time of growth, recession, inflation? Is it a time for optimism or pessimism? Next, the company's general marketing objectives must be considered. Does the company aim to increase or maintain its market share? Is it aggressively pursuing growth? Is it introducing a new product or promoting an established one? Is it pioneering, or is it responding to a change in the competition? Situation analysis ends with observations about problems with and opportunities for promoting a specific brand.

The purpose of market research is to solve a problem or exploit an opportunity. For a marketing communicator, a problem might be, "Our sales in the Southeast have dropped. Will increased advertising in local newspapers help?" An opportunity might be, "Our competition's market share decreased in the last year. What promotional activity would help us take advantage of the situation?"

Research is the gathering and analyzing of relevant data. "Relevant" is the key word. Facts and figures are generally abundant and not difficult to secure. Much more difficult is selecting useful data, those that relate to the success of a particular brand. Such research can be time-consuming and expensive, but it is usually worth the cost.

Sources of data

Two sources of data are available: secondary and primary. *Secondary data* are information that has already been gathered for some other purpose. It may be internal (within the company) or external (outside the company). A company's own sales records and accounts are excellent sources of internal secondary data. They are usually easy to obtain, and they can be extremely useful. Government census figures provide external secondary data. In some countries there are commercial sources of information, too. A disadvantage of secondary data is that they may not be relevant. They tell only what happened in the past, and they may be out of date. Secondary research can indicate sales trends in a product category. It can tell how many people have bought a product. But it cannot explain why they bought it. And consumer motivation is an increasingly important consideration in advertising.

Primary data are collected for the first time for a specific market research study. There are two kinds of primary research: qualitative (exploratory, or subjective) and quantitative (conclusive, or objective). The purpose of *qualitative research* is to obtain a general feeling about the market, the consumer, or the product. It is not to reach specific conclusions. An example of qualitative research is the depth interview, in which one consumer is questioned extensively. A disadvantage of qualitative research is that the sampling is necessarily very small. Quan-

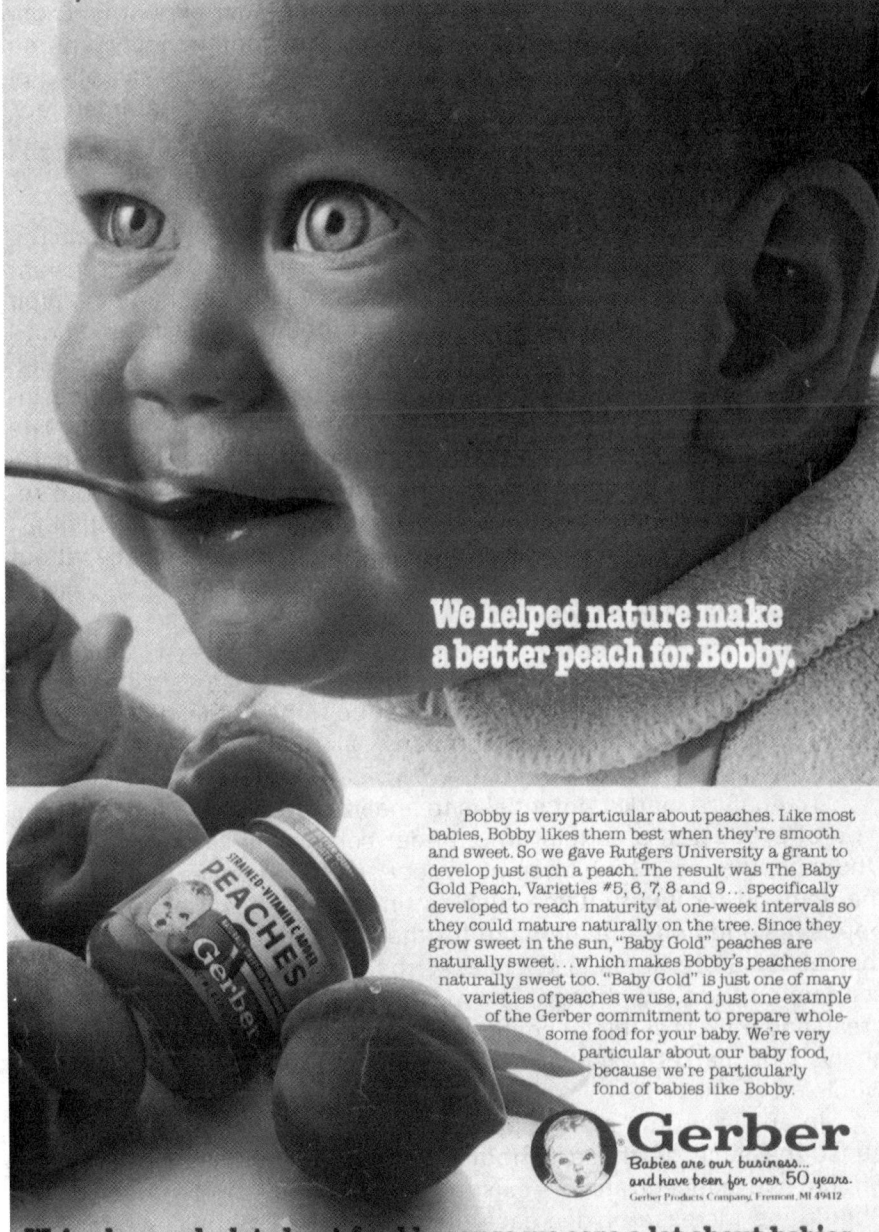

We helped nature make a better peach for Bobby.

Bobby is very particular about peaches. Like most babies, Bobby likes them best when they're smooth and sweet. So we gave Rutgers University a grant to develop just such a peach. The result was The Baby Gold Peach, Varieties #5, 6, 7, 8 and 9...specifically developed to reach maturity at one-week intervals so they could mature naturally on the tree. Since they grow sweet in the sun, "Baby Gold" peaches are naturally sweet...which makes Bobby's peaches more naturally sweet too. "Baby Gold" is just one of many varieties of peaches we use, and just one example of the Gerber commitment to prepare wholesome food for your baby. We're very particular about our baby food, because we're particularly fond of babies like Bobby.

Gerber

Babies are our business... and have been for over 50 years.

Gerber Products Company, Fremont, MI 49412

We've learned a lot about food because we care a lot about babies.

titative primary data are gathered by three methods: experiment, observation, and survey. The consumer survey is by far the most common method used in planning an advertising campaign. A wide sampling of the population is surveyed, by mail, telephone, or personal interview. The survey will generally help to determine which advertising message to use, and which is the likely audience for it. *Quantitative research* aims for definite conclusions.

Once the data (primary or secondary, internal or external, qualitative or quantitative) are gathered, they are analyzed. Useful, relevant information is extracted and can be used to solve the problem or exploit the opportunity that began the study. With today's sophisticated computers, typical marketing research methods are becoming obsolete. More and more companies are using a computer-based marketing information system *(MIS)* for help in making marketing decisions. The MIS can overcome the disadvantages of traditional research. Properly used, it will produce only relevant data, analyze information about recurrent problems, and encourage coordination of all research activities. An up-to-date MIS can provide information regularly, even daily, about past performance, present conditions, and future trends. It can be invaluable in planning an advertising campaign.

Areas of market research

Market research (situation analysis) must be done in these areas: market potential or industry sales, company sales, market share, distribution, and advertising costs.

To analyze market potential is to analyze the demand for a specific type of product at a certain time, under certain marketing conditions. Under conditions of high unemployment and rising prices, for example, the demand for luxury items such as fine furniture will be low. Under opposite conditions, the demand for the same items will increase. The market for these items is volatile; it changes dramatically as general economic conditions change. The market for goods in daily use, such as bread and milk, is stable; it changes little with economic conditions. The analysis of market potential reveals sales figures for an industry as a whole.

In analyzing the market potential, the advertiser considers broad questions such as these: Should we be pessimistic or optimistic? Should we concentrate on existing markets or look for new ones? Should we increase or decrease our advertising? Should we raise or lower our prices? The study of industry sales provides tentative answers to these questions. That's just a start.

The next step is to study sales for individual companies. The goal is still to isolate problems and opportunities. Current company sales should be compared to earlier ones, to determine trends. They should also be compared to competitors' sales, past and present.

Analysis of industry sales and company sales together provides information about market share, or brand share. Market share indicates the performance of a specific brand in relation to a competitor's brand, and to the industry as a whole. A major difficulty with brand share analysis is that it shows only relative market position and changes in that position. It does not show why those changes are taking place. Further analysis of the figures is necessary.

Distribution is the next area of research. Four kinds of index are used in analysis of distribution. The first two are often based on distribution by geographical area. In both, the index is based on an arbitrary scale of 100. The brand-development index (BDI) compares sales of a specific brand and total sales in the product category. (In the Southeast, the BDI for Cereal Brand X was 117. In the Northeast, it was 73.) The category-development index (*CDI*) compares sales in the product category and sales in the region. (In the Northeast, the CDI for all cereals was 92. In the Southeast, it was 94.) A comparison of the BDI and CDI shows that Cereal Brand X is doing poorly in the Northeast and well in the Southeast. *Store-count distribution* refers to the number of stores that carry a brand. For example, 89.1% of all grocery stores carry Cereal Brand X. All-commodity volume *(ACV)* refers to the total amount of sales in a category, for example, sales of all cereals in all grocery stores. A few stores have a high volume of sales. Most stores have a low sales volume. Therefore, it is possible to achieve high distribution by selling a product in only a few stores—those with high sales volume.

The next area for research and analysis is costs of advertising and merchandising, both for the company and for the competition. Ideally, market share ought to reflect advertising share. Suppose that five companies are selling a similar product. Together, they make up 100% of the market for that product. They account for 100% of the advertising expenditure for it. If one company spends 50% of the total advertising expenditure but has only 10% of the market, something is wrong. That company needs to study its advertising costs and effectiveness. The nature of competitors' advertising should also be studied. What are its form and content? What claims does it make for the product? Are they unique and valid? Which consumers are the target audience for the other companies' promotional efforts?

Discussion

1. What is the basis for marketing communication?
2. How does an advertising campaign begin?

3. What are the areas of market research?

4. How does situation analysis begin? How does it end?

5. How would you define marketing? What is the relationship between advertising, merchandising, and marketing?

6. Define *research*. What is the purpose of market research?

7. Find a printed advertisement and tell how it communicates, informs, and persuades.

8. Do you agree that "marketing begins with a consumer need"? Give some arguments against the idea.

9. How does competition bring about an abundance and variety of consumer goods?

10. Do you agree that the market is "people who have money and are ready to spend it"?

11. The concept that marketing is a response to consumers' needs is relatively new. What do you think marketing used to be like?

12. What should an advertiser know about its competition's advertising?

13. What is the broad economic picture in your country at this time?

14. Give additional examples of problems and opportunities that situation analysis might reveal for a company. How can both problems and opportunities give a company positive direction?

15. A company's sales records and accounts are sources of internal secondary data. What other sources can you think of?

16. What kinds of external secondary data are available in your country? From what sources?

17. What are some disadvantages of secondary data? Why are primary data usually more useful?

18. Explain, with examples, the difference between qualitative and quantitative research. What is a major disadvantage of qualitative research?

19. What are some advantages of an MIS over traditional research methods?

20. Explain market potential.

21. Name several products whose market in your country is volatile.

Name others whose market is stable.

22. How is market share (brand share) determined? Why is it useful for a company to know its own market share and the market shares of its competitors? When can market share figures be misleading?

23. Show that you understand BDI, CDI, store-count distribution, and ACV by giving an example of each for another product.

24. How is it possible to achieve high distribution while selling in a small number of stores? Give examples of such stores in your country.

25. What should market share reflect?

Review

Fill in the blanks with appropriate words from the text.

1. A _____ may be a consumer good, an industrial good, a service, or an idea.

2. To the average person, advertising is any kind of _____.

3. In the vocabulary of marketing, advertising is paid promotion in the four major _____.

4. _____ supplements advertising. It takes the forms of sales promotion and promotion in minor media.

5. Marketing begins with a consumer _____.

6. Marketing societies have produced a great abundance and variety of consumer goods, by means of _____.

7. The _____ is people who have money and are ready to spend it.

8. Successful producers are guided by the marketing _____: response to consumers' needs.

9. The purpose of market research is to solve a _____ or exploit an opportunity.

10. Research is the gathering and analyzing of _____ data.

11. Research data can be _____ or secondary.

12. Secondary data can be internal or _____.

13. Secondary data can indicate sales _____ in a product category.

14. _____ data are gathered by experiment, observation, and survey.

15. _____ research aims for definite conclusions.

16. The market for luxury goods is volatile. The market for goods in daily use is _____.

17. Analysis of industry sales and company sales together provides information about _____ (_____) _____.

18. Four kinds of index are used in analyzing _____.

19. The _____ index compares sales of a specific brand and total sales in the product category.

20. _____ refers to the total amount of sales in a product category.

The Consumer

Special Terms

Motive
> A desire that moves a consumer to act upon a need. The motive for a purchasing decision may be conscious or unconscious, rational or emotional.

Rational
> Based on intellect and reason.

Emotional
> Based on feeling.

Perception
> How a person perceives sense stimuli. Perception is subjective and selective.

Attitude
> A person's opinion or feeling about someone or something.

Meaning
> A learning theory principle, used to relate advertising content to consumers in a personal way.

Contiguity
> Another learning theory principle. In advertising, it is used to associate the product with an agreeable situation.

Reward
> Another principle of learning theory. It is used in advertising that promises favorable results from product use.

Repetition
> A fourth principle of learning theory. In advertising, it is the reiteration of a brand name or an advertisement.

Reference group
> A group to which someone may or may not belong, but to which one refers for guidance. It helps to form one's values, opinions, and behavior.

Social class

A stratum of society. One's membership in a social class is based on such factors as family background, occupation, and education.

Culture

The pattern of behavior, values, and attitudes transmitted from one generation to another.

Market segmentation

Dividing the market into homogeneous subgroups, for the purpose of making marketing more efficient by focusing on appropriate target markets.

Demographics

Classification of consumers according to facts about the population, such as population density, per capita income, and ethnic background.

Psychographics

Classification of consumers according to such factors as way of life and personality traits.

Family life cycle

A concept that identifies consumers by age, marital status, and number and ages of children.

Heavy-user theory

The theory that a relatively small proportion of consumers use a relatively large proportion of certain products.

Vocabulary Practice

1. What is the difference between a *motive* and a need? Give four words that describe consumers' purchasing motives.

2. Which is based on intellect, a *rational* motive or an *emotional* motive?

3. What kind of stimuli are subject to *perception?* Give two words that describe perception.

4. Define *attitude.*

5. Explain how *meaning* is used in advertising.

6. How is *contiguity* used in advertising?

7. In what type of advertising is *reward* used?

8. What is *repetition?*

9. What is a *reference group?* What do reference groups help to form?

10. Give at least two bases for determining *social class.*

11. Define *culture.*

12. What is the purpose of *market segmentation?*

13. What is the difference between *demographics* and *psychographics?* Into which category does ethnic background fit? Per capita income?

14. How does the *family life cycle* identify consumers?

15. Explain the *heavy-user theory.*

The Consumer

Consumer motivation

Modern marketing begins with the consumer. A consumer's decision to buy a product is an attempt to solve a problem or satisfy a need. In a competitive marketing economy, each manufacturer wants to inform consumers about its product and motivate them to buy it. Therefore, marketing communicators need to understand some basic theories of consumer motivation.

One is that purchasing *motives* may be conscious or unconscious. Brands in the same category are often very similar. Sometimes there is a considerable difference in price. Many consumers will buy the more expensive brand. If they are asked why, they might say, "Because this one tastes better." That is conscious motivation for the choice. But there is often an unconscious motivation, too. It might be that they want to impress their friends, or that it is the product their parents used. They may not want people to think they can't afford the more expensive brand. It is likely that unconscious motives are even more important and powerful than conscious ones. For effective advertising, it is desirable to try to determine both kinds of motive.

Another distinction is often made between *rational* and *emotional* motives. The advertiser might appeal to either or both. In its advertising, Sears appeals to reason: "You can count on Sears service to follow you when you move." "You can count on Sears for credit when you need it." Coca-Cola™ appeals to emotion, with its slogan, "Have a Coke™ and a smile."

In 1954, A.H. Maslow first wrote about his theory of human needs. He said that they form a hierarchy, or pyramid. At the bottom of the pyramid are physical needs. Above them are social needs; then the needs for safety and esteem; and, at the top, the need for self-actualiza-

What's the NEW Thermo Bottle kids will be taking to school?

In lunchrooms across the country kids will be having fun…

"popping" the top of *Aladdin's* new Thermo Bottle…

inserting a straw, and drinking right out of it. No mess, no spills…

Plus—it's the only Thermo Bottle you can eat or drink right out of…

in the school kits with characters kids love most: Dukes of Hazzard, Strawberry Shortcake, Disney, and the new, soft fabric tote, LUNCHKINS.™

Look for the display with Popeye— and the POP-TOP.

SCHOOL LUNCH KITS

Aladdin Industries, Inc., Nashville, TN 37210

tion. The urge to meet needs provides motivation. According to Maslow, the basic physical needs, such as food and drink, must be met before needs at the next level can emerge. Furthermore, when one set of needs is satisfied, another must emerge; man's needs can never be fully satisfied.

Maslow's theory applies to the marketing concept. A population whose needs are physical will not require luxury automobiles, for example. Those may satisfy the higher need for esteem. In less developed economies, the greatest proportion of needs are at the bottom of the hierarchy. In more developed economies, those basic needs are generally satisfied. A greater proportion of products fulfills needs toward the top of the pyramid. Knowing the level of need of a target population helps the advertiser in planning a motivational appeal.

Internal variables of consumer behavior
According to psychological theory, consumer behavior is influenced by internal and external variables. Knowledge of these variables can help marketing communicators to create successful advertising.

Internal variables include perception, attitude, and learning. *Perception* is an individual's way of interpreting what he sees, hears, touches, smells, or tastes. His way will be very different from another person's. Perception is subjective, entirely within one person's mind. Two people may look at the same car. One sees its color and style. The other sees its capacity and construction. One buys and the other doesn't, although both may have similar transportation requirements and ability to pay. Perception is also selective. At any moment, we are surrounded by hundreds of stimuli, by sights, sounds, and other sensations. But the human mind can perceive only one stimulus at a time. The mind selects those that are most important, or that it is most ready for. One task of advertising is to communicate product image, that is, to have consumers perceive the product, subjectively, in a certain way. Another is to get their attention, to have them select the desired stimuli.

Attitudes have three components: feelings toward an object (such as a product), knowledge about the object, and readiness to behave toward the object in a certain way. The three components are generally consistent with each other. Someone who has favorable feelings toward a product is more likely to learn about it and to buy it. This is an extremely important principle in advertising. If a person has unfavorable feelings toward a product, and those can be changed to positive feelings, his or her entire attitude is likely to change. The potential consumer will be much more inclined to study and buy the product. Similarly, increasing someone's knowledge of the product, or inducing one to try it for the first time, will also influence the other components of one's attitude. Advertising that affects all three components increases the probability of changing attitudes. Therefore, most advertisers combine all three approaches in their appeals. They try to create favorable feelings, give information, and promote purchasing at the same time.

A knowledge of learning theory can also be applied effectively in advertising and merchandising. Four principles are of particular importance: meaning, contiguity, reward, and repetition. The principle of *meaning* is used to relate something in an advertisement to the consumer in a personal way. "Would you like a 14K gold chain for $8?" is meaningful to the person who would indeed like a gold chain. "If you are a tall or big man . . . here's a great-looking knit that fits!" is meaningful to a tall or big man. The principle of contiguity is used when, in an advertisement, the product is pictured in a particular situation. The situation illustrates a mood or quality which the producer wants the consumer to associate with the product. An example is someone smoking a cigarette in a beautiful mountain setting.

The *reward* principle is employed in an advertisement promising favorable results from using the product: "Scope in the new plastic bottle takes care of morning breath and morning fumbles." Of the four learning principles, *repetition* is perhaps the most used. The brand name might be repeated frequently in the advertisement; the same advertisement might appear on television several times in one evening.

External variables of consumer behavior

External variables that influence consumer behavior are social and cultural in nature. Man is a social being. Our need to be accepted as a member of a group is very strong, although often unconscious. Our values, opinions, and behavior are heavily influenced by groups to which we belong. Because we refer to these groups for guidance, they are called *reference groups.* We are also influenced by groups to which we would like to belong. Advertising often appeals to this characteristic. Many food products, for example, are displayed in the setting of a neighborhood picnic, a group of friends at the beach, or a family reunion. Sports and film celebrities frequently act as reference individuals in testimonial advertising; fans may buy a particular product because they identify with the celebrity promoting it.

Besides belonging, or wanting to belong, to groups, everyone is a member of both a social class and a culture. *Social class* is generally determined by family background, occupation, source (not amount) of income, location and type of house, and education. Members of the same social class will share similar values and spend their money in similar ways. Advertising appeals, particularly in specialized magazines catering to wrestlers or gourmet diners, for example, are often directed toward a specific social class.

Culture is the set of attitudes, customs, values, ways of perceiving, and behavior handed down from one generation to another. Cultural traits include how people dress; how men and women, and children

and adults, behave toward each other; what foods are eaten and how they are prepared; which forms of entertainment and recreation are favored; how a home ought to be furnished and decorated. Many countries have a dominant culture with significant subculture populations. These subcultures require specialized marketing communications. Where the values of these consumers differ from those of the dominant culture, communication with them must be in their own terms.

Market segmentation

"Know your prospects" is the first cardinal rule of advertising. The "prospects" are the target group of consumers. They are the people most likely to buy the product and to be satisfied with it. The major instrument for reaching the right audience is *market segmentation*. The total market is divided into homogeneous subgroups. Then the advertising campaign is directed toward a particular market segment.

For market segmentation, consumers are analyzed and defined in three ways: demographically, psychographically, and geographically. *Demographic* data are measurable facts; they are generally available from census reports. Useful demographic data include information about number of total population, rate of population growth, population density, per capita income, marital status, spending patterns, employment, ethnic origin, age, and education. Demographic information might, for example, suggest an advertising campaign aimed at married people of thirty to forty-five years of age, with a high school education and an income of under $15,000 a year. A campaign would be very different for single people under thirty, with a college education and an income over $25,000 a year. Demographic facts usually receive the most emphasis in market segmentation, because they are the easiest to obtain and measure.

However, especially as people become able to spend more on luxuries, *psychographics* become more important. They deal with both the quantity and quality of prospects. The potential market is segmented according to such factors as way of life and personality traits. Some people like to stay at home and watch television; others prefer more active outside entertainment. Some are careful shoppers who look for bargains; others buy on impulse, or because of a brand's prestige as they perceive it. Psychographic data cut across demographic lines. For instance, according to income, a grocery store clerk and a classical musician might be in the same demographic category. Psychographically, they are likely to be very different in their values, attitudes, and purchasing patterns. Demographics show what people do. Psychographics are concerned with why they do it. Thus psychographics more clearly show the relation between consumer and product.

The *family life cycle* combines demographic and psychographic

Handy answers to hard questions asked by children in the Health-tex years.

What is a diet?

Your diet is the food you eat. It's important to eat the foods that can keep your body the healthiest, especially while you're growing—and most especially if you're a pre-schooler because you're growing extra fast.

All food is made up of nutrients. Nutrients are anything that provides nourishment for your body. Nutrients are proteins, carbohydrates (sugar and starch), fats, vitamins and minerals. Your body changes proteins, carbohydrates and fats into energy. The amount of energy your body gets from food is measured in calories. Some nutrients also enable your body to replace worn-out cells, which is what makes you grow. You need over forty different nutrients to stay healthy, so it's important to eat a wide variety of foods to be sure you get every kind of nutrient.

Of course, when some people say they're going on "a diet," they mean that they are eating less, or eating special combinations of food, so they'll lose weight. But leaving out any of the basic food groups may hurt the dieter's health. Simply eating smaller amounts will keep most people at their proper weight—and even healthier than if they ate big quantities. People who get lots of exercise can eat more food without gaining weight, because the body uses up calories during exercise.

Eating good food is the most important way to feel good. Wearing nice clothes makes you feel good, too. Health-tex knows the clothes you need for back-to-school. The perfect cut—trim and comfortable. Handsomely color-coordinated tops and bottoms, including sweaters. Sturdy fabrics and craftsmanship. All for boys and girls sizes 3 months to 14.

Health·tex®

you eat two or more foods from each of the first four basic groups every day, and moderate amounts from group five, you have a healthy diet.

1. Milk, cheese and yogurt

2. Meats, poultry, fish, eggs, nuts, dried beans and peas, peanut butter

3. Vegetables and fruits—citrus fruits, salads, spinach, carrots, bananas, apples

4. Breads (whole-grain or enriched), cereals and pasta

5. Butter and fortified margarine or vegetable oil

approaches to market segmentation. It identifies potential consumers by age, marital status, and number and ages of children. It also implies differences in their attitudes and habits.

Family Life Cycle
1. Bachelor stage: young single individuals
2. Full nest: young married couples with children
   a. youngest child under six
   b. youngest child six or over
   c. older married couples with dependent children
3. Empty nest: older married couples with no children at home
4. Solitary survivors: older single or widowed people

Geographic analysis can reveal striking dissimilarities in consumer attitudes and patterns of consumption. In the United States, surveys show that certain products sell much better in some areas than in others: dinnerware in the Northeast, fishing poles in the Midwest, home freezers in the Southeast, and sleeping bags in the Northwest. Favorite colors vary: blue and white in the Northeast; yellow and orange in the Southeast; yellow, orange, and pink in the West; blue, green, and brown in the Northwest.

Some marketing communicators subscribe to the *"heavy-user" theory,* which cuts across all three lines of market segmentation. According to this theory, a relatively small proportion of consumers use a relatively large proportion of certain products. Advertising aimed toward the heavy users is considered unusually efficient. A recent refinement of the heavy-user theory is the 80/20% rule. In the United States, researchers have discovered that in several product categories— including dog food, instant coffee, and beer—20% of the buyers purchase 80% of the goods. And 20% of telephone customers make 80% of the calls. The figures are remarkably consistent.

Essential to all of these theories and practices is the marketing concept: marketing, advertising, and merchandising begin and end with the consumer.

Discussion

1. What does a consumer's purchasing decision try to do?

2. Why should marketing communicators understand motivation theory?

3. The text gives examples of conscious and unconscious motives for buying a more expensive brand. The relative cost of similar brands

is one way to illustrate differences in motives. What are some of the others?

4. Name two other types of motives. Which do you think is more important in advertising?

5. Which motives would an ad for cosmetics be more likely to appeal to? An ad for an investment firm? An ad for a cruise?

6. Find a printed advertisement that you think appeals to both conscious and unconscious motives. Identify them.

7. Find advertisements that appeal to reason, to emotion, and to both reason and emotion.

8. Why is the pyramidal form of Maslow's hierarchy of needs significant?

9. Do you agree with the order of Maslow's hierarchy? Do you agree that "man's needs can never be fully satisfied"?

10. Do you live in a marketing society? At what level of needs is the majority of the population in your country? What does this tell you about applying the marketing concept there?

11. Hold up any object for two classmates. Ask them to describe it. Then let them hold it and describe it again. How do their perceptions differ?

12. How is perception important in advertising?

13. "The three components (of attitudes) are generally consistent with each other." Explain.

14. Find advertisements that use the principles of meaning, contiguity, reward, and repetition.

15. Talk about groups to which you belong (they don't have to be formally organized) that help to influence your values, opinions, and behavior. How does their influence differ, in nature and in strength?

16. Talk about groups you don't belong to that influence you. Are there any people who are reference individuals for you?

17. Are there distinctions of social class in your country? If so, on what are they based? Name some characteristics of the different classes. Consider such factors as preferences in entertainment, food, style of clothing, way of speech, educational institutions, and type of housing.

18. Discuss the dominant culture of your country. The text gives you several subjects for discussion, beginning with how people dress.

Find advertising that reflects the dominant culture. Explain in what ways it does so.

19. Does your country have significant subculture populations? Identify them. How do they differ from the dominant culture? Find advertising that is directed toward them. Or take an advertisement directed toward the dominant culture and describe how you would modify it for subcultures.

20. What sources of demographic data are available to you?

21. The text gives two examples of directing an advertising campaign toward different demographic groups. Tell how the two campaigns might be different, using your own example of the product advertised.

22. Give more examples of psychographic data. Why are psychographics more important as people can spend more on luxuries?

23. Study the family life cycle. Talk about the kinds of consumer goods that would most interest people at the various stages.

24. Discuss geographical differences in consumption patterns in your country.

25. Does the heavy-user theory apply to your area? The 80/20% rule?

Review

Mark T (True) or F (False) for each statement, according to the information in the text.

_____ 1. Modern marketing begins with the producer.

_____ 2. Consumers are always aware of their reasons for buying a product.

_____ 3. Unconscious purchasing motives are probably more important and powerful than conscious ones.

_____ 4. Some motives are rational, some are emotional.

_____ 5. According to Maslow, the most basic human needs are social.

_____ 6. A person's needs can never be fully satisfied.

_____ 7. Perception, attitude, and learning are internal variables of consumer behavior.

_____ 8. Perception is subjective and selective.

_____ 9. A person can perceive only one stimulus at a time.

_____ 10. The three components of attitudes are generally consistent with one another.

_____ 11. Most advertisers combine appeals to all three components in their advertising.

_____ 12. Associating the product with an agreeable situation is using the learning principle of meaning.

_____ 13. An advertisement that promises favorable results from using the product employs the principle of reward.

_____ 14. The principle of contiguity is probably used more than the other three principles of learning.

_____ 15. One must belong to a reference group to be influenced by it.

_____ 16. One's culture is determined partly by one's family background.

_____ 17. There is no point in advertising to subcultures of a population.

_____ 18. Demographic data are measurable facts about a population.

_____ 19. Demographic data become more important as more people are able to buy luxuries.

_____ 20. In the empty nest stage of the family life cycle, no children are living at home.

The Product

Special Terms

Image
> How consumers perceive a company, product, or brand; the mental picture its name evokes.

Strategy of concentration
> An approach to market segmentation in which the marketing effort is directed toward one large population subgroup.

Strategy of differentiation
> An approach to market segmentation in which two or more subgroups are identified and selected, and a marketing program is designed for each.

Product differentiation
> A marketing strategy in which a product is made to appear different from competitive products, by a change in the product or by advertising claim.

Product life cycle
> The four stages that a product typically goes through: introductory, growth, maturity, and decline.

Line extension
> The addition of a new product to an existing set.

Pioneering advertising
> Advertising that introduces a product to consumers.

Competitive advertising
> Advertising that stresses the superiority of one product over others in the category.

Retentive advertising
> Advertising designed to keep the brand in the public mind.

Brand awareness
> Consumers' knowledge that the brand exists.

Brand preference
Consumers' choice of the brand over other, similar ones.
Brand loyalty
Consumers' well-established preference for the brand. They continue to buy it despite possible advantages of competing brands.
Product feature
A physical characteristic of a product.
Benefit claim
How an advertiser says that a product will help a consumer.
Position
Benefit claim; also the place of a product in consumers' minds.
Product concept
The producer's idea of the product's principal value for consumers; the essential message of an advertising campaign.

Vocabulary Practice

1. Define *image.*

2. What is a *strategy of concentration?*

3. What is a *strategy of differentiation?*

4. What is *product differentiation?* Describe two ways of making a product appear different.

5. Name the four stages in the *product life cycle,* in the correct order.

6. Define *line extension.*

7. What is the function of *pioneering advertising?*

8. What does *competitive advertising* emphasize?

9. What is the purpose of *retentive advertising?*

10. Define *brand awareness, brand preference,* and *brand loyalty.* Make clear the differences among them.

11. What is a *product feature?*

12. What is a *benefit claim?*

13. Give two definitions for *position.*

14. What is the *product concept?*

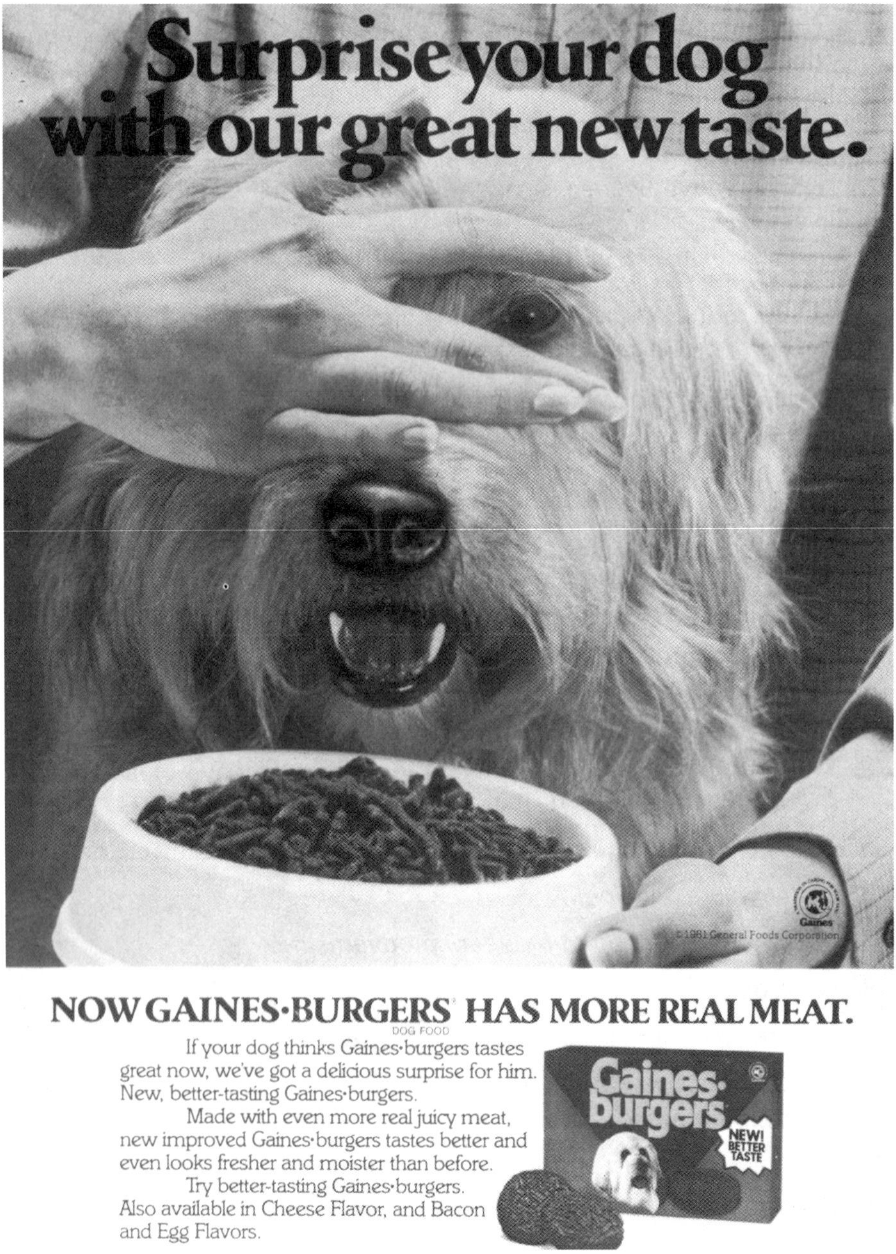

Surprise your dog with our great new taste.

NOW GAINES·BURGERS HAS MORE REAL MEAT.
DOG FOOD

If your dog thinks Gaines·burgers tastes great now, we've got a delicious surprise for him. New, better-tasting Gaines·burgers.

Made with even more real juicy meat, new improved Gaines·burgers tastes better and even looks fresher and moister than before.

Try better-tasting Gaines·burgers. Also available in Cheese Flavor, and Bacon and Egg Flavors.

The Product

What is a product?
After "Know your prospects," the second cardinal rule of advertising and merchandising is "Know your product." "Product" needs definition. Is an insurance policy a product? Is a bank account a product? Is "Drive 55—Save Lives"? Is "Protect endangered species"? Yes. Services and ideas are products. They serve consumers, and they are advertised. They are subjects of communication between "consumers" and "producers." Insurance companies, banks, organizations, and interest groups have *images,* just as brands of soup and soap do. Many books, including this one, tend to treat only consumer goods as products. It should be remembered that what is said here generally applies to services and ideas as well.

A retail store is a product, too. Like goods, services, and ideas, a retail store has an image in consumers' minds. It serves consumers, it is advertised, it communicates, it has an identity. Studies show that consumers are at least as loyal to a store as they are to a particular product or brand. They choose a store for such reasons as location, convenience, appearance, cleanliness, quality and variety of goods, politeness of employees, availability of desired goods, price, and even atmosphere.

Another way of defining a product is to say that someone who buys a product actually buys three: the identifiable product, the service and warranty that go with it, and the purchaser's expectations of product performance. Marketing communicators need to be aware that they are addressing a whole complex of consumer interests.

Market segmentation and product differentiation
How can a product best be matched to consumers' expectations, so that it meets their needs? One method is market segmentation, discussed in the previous unit. Its significance for the product can be seen in the two approaches to market segments. In a *strategy of concentration,* the marketing effort is directed toward a sizable subgroup of the population, such as working mothers of young children. Products are manufactured and marketed to meet their particular needs. In a *strategy of differentiation,* two or more subgroups are identified and selected. A marketing program is designed for each. Car manufacturers differentiate according to income level. They produce cars in several different price ranges. Cereal boxes come in various sizes, to suit families at different stages of the family life cycle. Shampoo is made for people with "normal," "dry," and "oily" hair.

The second method of reaching target consumers is *product differentiation.* Here, the marketing effort is directed toward the total market, not just a segment of it. The difference is in the product, not in the market. The success of this method depends upon an appeal to consumers' perceptions. Today's large supermarkets will have 25,000 different brands and products. A typical drugstore might have 40,000. Where competition is that intense, a number of products will be very similar, except for brand. The consumer has no strong reason to prefer one to another. Therefore, to compete, a product must be seen as different in some way. One method is to change the product visibly, so that it is perceived as unique. The change may make no difference in product performance. A simple change in color might be enough. Another method is to make unique advertising claims. These might support the physical change. When Joy dishwashing liquid added the scent of lemons, it advertised "new lemon-fresh Joy." Another kind of claim could be true for any similar product, but it is made in an original and memorable way, just as Savarin is "the coffee-er coffee."

However, a product difference means nothing to consumers unless they perceive it. They care about how it will affect them, that it will make them look better, feel better, or live longer. Advertisers must be sure that consumers not only understand a product difference but see it as a benefit. The difference need not be in the tangible product alone. Consumers' perceptions of the company, the store, the brand, the price, the package, and the advertising itself all influence their attitudes toward a product. Changes in any of these also signal product differentiation in their minds.

The product life cycle

An important use of product differentiation is to extend the *product life cycle.* According to the life cycle theory, a product goes through four stages: introduction, growth, maturity, and decline. Each stage has implications for marketing communicators.

Not only completely new products have an introductory phase. A new process, such as freeze-dried coffee, will also go through the four stages. So will an addition to a line, such as an economy model of a major appliance, a new flavor of ice cream, or a new form of dog biscuit. In the introductory stage, growth is slow, prices are high, and advertising expenditures are high relative to sales—consumers must first be made aware of the product before they can even consider trying it for the first time.

During the growth period, sales rise quickly as some customers buy the product for the first time, and others buy it again. As potential competitors see the increase in profits, more begin to enter the field. Market segmentation and product differentiation come into use. Major improvements are made in the product, and new forms of it appear. Merchandising activities increase. Advertising expense is still high in total volume, but lower in relation to sales.

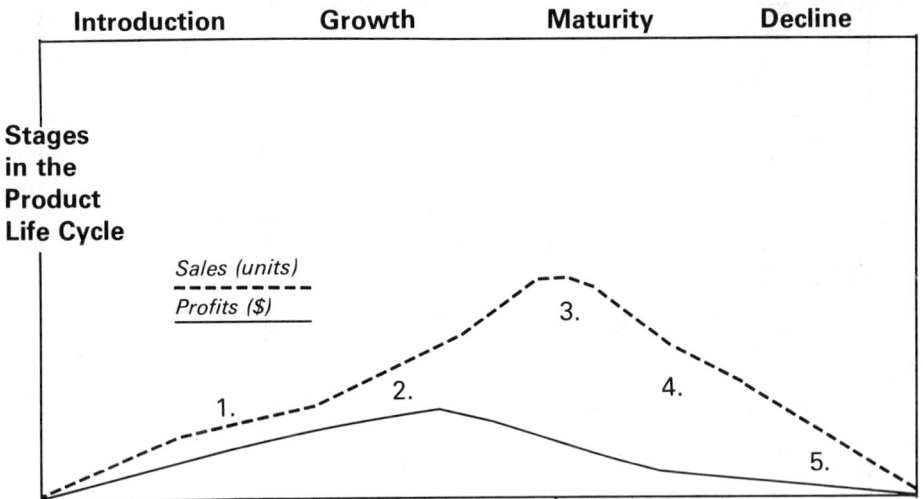

| Introduction | Growth | Maturity | Decline |

Stages in the Product Life Cycle

1. Consumers gradually try the product. Initial costs of production and advertising are high. Therefore, prices are high.
   Sales growth is slow. *Profits* increase slowly.
2. Pioneering consumers use the product again, and new users join them. Prices decrease as demand and production increase.
   Sales growth increases. *Profits* increase, but less rapidly than sales.
3. As profits increase, competition increases. Prices drop further.
   Sales growth reaches a peak. The market is saturated.
   Profits begin to decline because of increased competition.
4. Because both *sales* and *profits* are declining, many competitors leave the field. Only the strongest remain.
5. The product is no longer useful. Manufacturers look for greater profits in other areas.
   Sales and therefore *profits* decline.

The maturity stage begins when most potential customers have already tried the product. Weaker competitors disappear; stronger ones survive. Growth slows, and prices and profits decrease. Any growth in sales will come through general population growth or at the expense of competitors. This stage continues much longer than the earlier ones. Most products on the market at any one time are in the maturity stage.

A product enters the decline period when new products replace old ones, or changes in consumption patterns eliminate demand. Industry sales drop, and manufacturers abandon the industry to look for more profitable products.

If action is taken early enough in the maturity phase, it is possible to extend the life of a product. One way of doing this is product differentiation. Another method is *line extension.* New products are added to an existing line to increase variety and therefore sales. Line extension may involve market segmentation, as when a bedding manufacturer adds bed linens for children to its line. It may not involve segmentation, as when Jell-o adds a new flavor. Other ways of extending the life of a product are to find new uses for old products and to add servicing to the product. Product difference depends upon consumers' perceptions. The

Nature of Advertising at Various Stages in the Product Life Cycle

Introduction	Growth	Maturity	Decline
Pioneering Aim: Brand Awareness	Competitive Aim: Brand Preference	Retentive Aim: Brand Loyalty	
[Attracts Customers to a New Product]	[Emphasizes Product Uniqueness & Superiority]	[Keeps Product's Existence in Consumers' minds]	

same is true of "new" products. Consumers will perceive a product as new if changes are made in the brand name, the package, or the price. "Newness" is a common device in advertising. "Oh, we don't use _____ anymore." "You don't! Why not?" "Because now there's new, improved _____!" However, the change must be perceived by the senses; a change in advertising claim is empty without a response in consumer perception.

The emphasis of advertising changes as a product goes through its life cycle. Advertising has pioneering, competitive, and retentive stages. In the *pioneering* stage, the product is introduced as a solution to old problems. The purpose of pioneering advertising is to tell consumers that the product exists and to make them eager to try it. In other words, it informs and creates *brand awareness.* In its *competitive* phase, advertising emphasizes superiority to competitors' products. The goal is *brand preference* and the establishment of *brand loyalty.* It is used during the growth and early maturity periods of the product life cycle. As the maturity stage continues, *retentive* advertising is most effective. By that time, consumers have accepted and preferred the product. Advertising in this period is designed chiefly to keep the brand in the public mind, to maintain *brand loyalty.*

Product analysis and positioning

Product analysis is like market analysis and consumer analysis. It means finding out everything possible about the subject—in this case, the product. It is a matter of collecting and analyzing relevant data. It involves studying the competition. To "know your product" (and your competitor's) is to know why people use it; how it is different; where it fits in the product life cycle. Knowing the product is knowing its uses and functions, quality, construction or composition, distribution patterns, packaging, brand image, and price. In product analysis, the overriding considerations are how the product compares to its competition and how it is positioned in consumers' minds.

"What does our product have that theirs lacks?" Equally important, "What does their product have that ours lacks?" A product has specific physical characteristics. Those are its *features.* The advertiser's job is to look for unique product features. What can this product do that others cannot? Is it easier to use? Cheaper? More pleasant to smell or taste or see? Does it work faster? Is it more reliable? Easier to find? When Crest toothpaste entered the market, it was unique. It was the only toothpaste that contained fluoride, and it had the approval of dentists. The makers of Crest were able to prove that it really did fight cavities. They had figures that would persuade the public.

The uniqueness of a product feature is not enough, however. Consumers must perceive it as unique. And they must see it as a benefit. What they really want to know is, "How will this product benefit me?"

"You can feel it when you drive."

Lee Trevino

NEW BRIDGESTONE SUPERFILLER RADIALS.

The Bridgestone Tire Company announces new SuperFiller steel-belted radial tires.

Bridgestone's advancements in tire technology have resulted in a radial tire that gives you premium performance.

("How will it solve my problem or satisfy my need?") A major purpose of product analysis is to discover and exploit product benefit. Directing the *benefit claim* to consumers is the attempt to "position" the product. "Position" has traditionally been defined as the product's benefit claim. Its more modern definition centers on the consumer: A product's "position" is its place in consumers' minds. It is their perception of the product. This position is usually achieved by advertising.

For a new product, correct positioning is a vital aspect of product analysis and is basic to an advertising campaign. It is no less vital and basic for an established product, but the approach is different. For an existing product, its current position must first be analyzed. Then the campaign planner may decide that the product has to be repositioned, for better sales. Example: Arm and Hammer baking soda had been on the market for many years. Its major uses were in cooking and for soothing upset stomachs. Then the manufacturers began advertising it as a deodorizer, and sales skyrocketed. They had succeeded in repositioning the product in the minds of consumers.

Advertising campaign planners use the results of market analysis, consumer analysis, and product analysis to develop a *product concept.* It is their idea of the principal value of the product for consumers. This is what they try to communicate. The product concept is at the heart of all advertising and merchandising. It is based on knowledge of the market, including the competition; understanding of the consumer; and knowledge of the product.

Discussion

1. How can a service be considered a product? An idea? Find examples of advertising for both.

2. How can a retail store be considered a product? Do you use certain stores regularly? Why?

3. What does a person "buy" along with an identifiable product?

4. Distinguish between the strategies of concentration and differentiation.

5. Give additional examples of the strategy of differentiation.

6. Distinguish between the strategy of differentiation and product differentiation.

7. Why has product differentiation become important? What are some ways to accomplish it? Give examples of product differentiation in your country.

8. Why isn't it enough for consumers to know about a product difference? What are some ways of signaling product difference to them?

9. How can product differentiation extend the product life cycle?

10. What, besides a completely new product, goes through an introductory stage?

11. Talk about growth, prices, and advertising expense in the introductory phase.

12. Discuss sales, profits, competition, market segmentation, product differentiation, merchandising, and advertising expense during the growth period.

13. How do competition, growth, price, profit, and sales change during the maturity stage?

14. How can the decline period be recognized? How does it affect an industry?

15. How can line extension increase the life of a product?

16. Give some examples of line extension that involve market segmentation, and some that do not.

17. How, besides product differentiation and line extension, can the product life cycle be extended?

18. Put these in the correct order and match each one with the corresponding stage of the product life cycle: competitive advertising, retentive advertising, and pioneering advertising.

19. Match brand loyalty, brand preference, and brand awareness with the three kinds of advertising.

20. List the things an advertiser should know about a product.

21. What are the two major considerations in product analysis?

22. Make a list of five familiar products. Discuss their features and their benefits as claimed in advertising.

23. Name as many recent unique products as you can.

24. Make a list of ten familiar brands. Read them to a classmate, one by one. Find out how each is positioned in your classmate's mind.

25. Name any examples of successful repositioning you can think of.

Review

Fill in the blanks with appropriate words from the text.

1. The cardinal rules of advertising are "Know your product" and "Know your _____."

2. The way in which consumers perceive a product is its _____.

3. Not all products are consumer _____.

4. Someone who buys a product buys the identifiable product, the service and warranty that go with it, and his or her _____ of product performance.

5. Two strategies of market segmentation are _____ and differentiation.

6. Automobile manufacturers differentiate according to consumers' level of _____.

7. Two ways of reaching target consumers are market segmentation and _____ _____.

8. Consumers must understand a product difference and perceive it as a _____.

9. In its life cycle, a product goes through four stages: introductory, _____, _____, and _____.

10. In the introductory stage, growth is _____ and prices are _____.

11. Most products on the market are in the _____ stage.

12. One way to extend the life of a product is product differentiation. Another way is _____ extension.

13. Advertising has pioneering, _____, and retentive stages.

14. Pioneering advertising informs and creates brand _____.

15. Retentive advertising is designed to maintain brand _____.

16. Product analysis includes studying the company's product and the product of the_____.

17. A product's physical characteristics are its _____.

18. Directing a benefit claim to consumers is _____.

19. Consumers' perception of a product is usually achieved by _____.

20. The _____ _____ is the advertiser's idea of the principal value of the product for consumers.

Price, Package, and Brand

Special Terms

Supply
> The quantity of a product available to consumers at a particular time.

Demand
> The quantity of a product desired by consumers at a particular time.

Surplus
> The quantity available above that desired by consumers.

Monopoly
> An economic situation in which one supplier controls the total supply of a necessary product.

Competition
> An economic situation in which there are many suppliers of the same product.

Monopolistic competition
> A situation in which each competing producer has a "monopoly" because no two products are identical.

Symbolic pricing
> A price fixed to convey a particular idea about a product to consumers, and not according to supply and demand or production costs.

Package
> The product itself, as in the case of major appliances and automobiles. In the case of most consumer goods, the container.

Design
> The use of typography, color, and photographs or illustrations on a package.

Product attributes

Characteristics of the product; both features and benefits.

Brand

A name, sign, symbol, design, term, or combination of these that differentiates one company's products from another's. One manufacturer's product, so distinguished from others in the category.

Brand name

The part of the brand that can be spoken.

Brand mark

The part of the brand that can be recognized but not spoken.

Trade name

The name under which a company operates.

Trademark

Any word or symbol that identifies the maker of a product. It is protected by law.

Brand-extension strategy

A technique by which the names of new products include the names of established ones.

Vocabulary Practice

1. What is *supply?*

2. What is *demand?*

3. What is a *surplus?*

4. Define *monopoly.*

5. Define *competition.*

6. How does *monopolistic competition* receive its name?

7. What is the purpose of *symbolic pricing?*

8. Give two definitions of *package.*

9. Name three elements of package *design.*

10. Name two categories of *product attributes.*

11. What is a *brand?* What is its function?

12. Define *brand name.* Distinguish between brand name and *brand mark.*

13. What is a *trade name?*

14. What is a *trademark* and how is it protected?
15. What is a *brand-extension strategy?*

Price, Package, and Brand

Price, package, and brand name are all subjects of research, and all help to communicate the product concept.

Price

Classic economic theory says that the importance of price is its relation to *supply* and *demand.* Price decreases, and demand increases, as more people can buy the product. Supply increases to meet the demand. But then, because of competition, profits also decrease. Some producers abandon the product because it is no longer profitable. This reduces the supply again; as a result, price increases. With the increase in price comes an increase in profitability and therefore in production. The cycle begins again.

However, the classic view is no longer completely valid. This is especially true in good economic times and in a more affluent industrial society. In such a society, demand increases for goods that were formerly luxuries. Levels of productivity are high, so there is always a *surplus* of many products. Manufacturers have to generate demand in order to sell their goods. In this situation, marketing must be oriented toward the consumer, not the producer. Consumer-oriented production leads to market segmentation and product differentiation. It has also led to the development of the newer concepts of monopolistic competition and symbolic pricing.

"Monopolistic competition" is a combination of "monopoly" and "competition." In a *monopoly,* a single supplier governs the total supply of a necessary product. In *competition,* there are many suppliers, and all of their products are the same. Probably neither condition exists in pure form. In *monopolistic competition,* every producer has a "monopoly." This is because no two manufacturers' products are exactly alike. If a consumer insists on smoking Marlboro cigarettes, he has to buy Marlboros. Winstons are cigarettes, too, but they are not identical. Today's marketing communicators try to persuade consumers that their own brands are unique. Each company tries to make it appear that it has a monopoly. The appearance of monopoly or uniqueness

thus becomes a feature of that company's product.

The function of *symbolic pricing* is to convey an idea to consumers. The price becomes a symbol, rather than just a reflection of supply and demand or of production costs. The saying "You get what you pay for" is firmly embedded in consumers' minds. A price that seems too low can actually slow demand, because it may indicate an inferior product to the mind of the consumer. The first home permanents cost twenty-five cents and were a failure. A new package and a new price of $1.25 made them successful. A price that seems high can increase demand because it suggests quality and desirability. Many people buy expensive brands to make themselves feel important and to impress others. In reality, studies show that there is little if any correlation between quality and price. Yet consumers believe that there is; and in a marketing society, they rule. Symbolic pricing is also effective for products whose quality cannot easily be judged by consumers. In the case of furniture, for example, potential buyers are heavily influenced by price and brand name reputation.

Because price says something to consumers, it is often a significant aspect of an advertising campaign.

Package

Packaging communicates, too. For many products, such as washers and dryers, furniture, clothing, and cars, the product itself is the *package.* The styling or design of the product receives a great deal of attention, from both producer and consumer. Equal attention should be paid to the design, as well as the function, of packages that contain goods. The original purpose of packaging was simply to store and protect the contents. For many consumer goods, the package has now become as important as the product—if not more so. The package may be the primary available advertising tool. It will probably have a very short life span. In time, most packages will be discarded. Meanwhile, they are perhaps the cheapest, most visible, most efficient, and most effective form of marketing communication. And, many people in marketing feel, the most undervalued and least exploited.

In creating a package, there are three groups of requirements to consider: those of the product, the distributor, and the consumer. The product requires protection from handling and spoilage. Distributors prefer packages that are easy to stack and equally attractive from more than one side. For consumers, the major requirement is convenience. The basic demand is for a package that is easy to open. In recent years, convenience has taken a wide variety of expanded forms. Waxed paper, Saran Wrap, and aluminum foil packages have a cutting edge. Betty Crocker's Snackin' Cake™ is mixed and baked right in the inner package. Frozen foods are cooked in their own serving trays, or boiled in their own plastic bags. As more people demand convenience foods, they also demand convenience packaging.

These are functional considerations for good packaging. A package must also inform. It should describe the contents and give any necessary instructions or warnings about their use. The package is an advertising and merchandising tool as well. Some supermarket shelves display fifty different brands of breakfast cereal. In that environment, the package may make the sale. At home, it is a constant reminder of the brand name and of *product attributes.* It can illustrate both features and benefits of the product. Through its *design,* or appearance, the package supports the brand image and the product concept.

The package material, shape, and size also carry messages. Expensive perfumes, electric razors, and jewelry frequently come in special packages that connote quality and elegance. Others, such as soft plastic shampoo bottles, say "safety and convenience" in the shower. The shape of the package may suggest masculinity (square, strong shapes) or femininity (rounded, soft shapes). "Giant economy" or "family" size boxes of laundry detergent appeal to consumers in the full nest stage of the family life cycle.

Special merchandising offers appear on many packages. All Betty Crocker products have coupons that can be redeemed for merchandise.

Cereal boxes often have coupons worth fifteen or twenty cents on the next purchase of that cereal. Bisquick and Hershey's Cocoa packages give recipes using the product and make cookbook offers. All of these increase the benefit of the product in consumers' minds.

Today, many products come in "decorator packs" and "decorator colors," so that they can be left in public view. Examples are facial tissues, liquid soaps in their own dispensers, and toilet articles. Avon products are outstanding in this respect. The containers are so unusual and desirable that many people buy the products because of their packaging. Avon bottles have become valuable to collectors.

The package for L'eggs stockings and pantyhose ("Our L'eggs fit your legs") is an example of packaging at its best. The package serves its basic function of protecting and storing the contents. It meets the requirements of distributors. L'eggs are sold only in retail stores, and the company provides its own display racks. The product is highly visible. The egg-shaped package is unique; its shape is related to the brand name. The packaging itself helps consumers to remember the product. The L'eggs package communicates the product concept simply, clearly, and in a completely original way. It does everything that a package ought to do.

Brand name

The choice of a brand name might be one of a marketing communicator's most important decisions. An appropriate, attention-getting, memorable brand name effectively communicates the product concept and stays in consumers' minds. Standard Oil Company of New Jersey spent $100,000,000 to find a corporate name. They wanted one with no meaning, so that they could build into the name their own meaning and image. A computer supplied 10,000 possible names, which research reduced to one. That name was tested in 169 languages and dialects to see if it had a negative meaning in any. (Standard Oil wanted to avoid the problems of Chevrolet's Nova and American Motors' Matador: "It doesn't go" [*no va*] and "killer" in Spanish.) The winner was Exxon, one of history's most successful brand names.

Some terms used in branding may require definition. A *brand* is a name, sign, symbol, design, term, or combination of those. It identifies one company's products and distinguishes them from a competitor's. A *brand name* is the part of the brand that can be spoken. A *brand mark* is the part of the brand that can be recognized but not spoken. The style of lettering on a Coca-Cola™ bottle is familiar throughout the world. That is the brand mark. The words "Coca-Cola"™ are the brand name. A *trade name* is the name under which a company operates: Procter and Gamble, Kimberly Clark, Xerox. In the United States a *trademark* is protected by law. It gives the seller sole rights to use a brand name or a brand mark. Both "Coca-Cola"™ and "Coke"™ are trademarks.

Our great name had one small problem.

So we made it smaller.

We have the kind of great hotels people don't forget.

Unfortunately, we had the kind of name people didn't remember.

So we changed it.

Of course, the Hotel St. Francis, The Arizona Biltmore, the Continental Plaza, and each of our more than 50 other very individual hotels will still have the same style and personality that made them famous.

That doesn't change.

But together they'll be known as the Westin Hotels.

It's a name destined to be as memorable as the hotels themselves.

And there's one more thing that hasn't changed.

For reservations call your travel agent, company travel department or 800-228-3000.

Exxon's way of choosing a brand name was unusual. Several other strategies are more common. Some companies use the company name with identification of the product: Kraft Barbecue Sauce, Kraft Mayonnaise, Kraft Salad Dressing. This strategy is used by well-established companies. The company name gives prestige and value to the individual products, which are of a similar type. Other manufacturers use the company name with a brand name: Polaroid One-Step™, Polaroid SX-70. The brand names indicate product differentiation; the company name ties them together. A third strategy is commonly employed by large corporations with several diverse product lines. They use a brand name with product identification. Thus Procter and Gamble (trade name) has its Duncan Hines (brand name) cake mixes in various flavors, such as German chocolate (product identification). These three are *brand-extension strategies.* An existing name extends to cover new products. Brand extension works best if the company has established an excellent reputation, and if the old and new product concepts are similar. A fourth naming strategy is to use brand name only. Procter and Gamble, for instance, is a highly respected company that underplays its size and diversity. It markets each laundry detergent as a separate entity. Tide, Cheer, and Bold are examples.

In general, a brand name should:
1. Be original and distinctive. It should not imitate an existing name.
2. Be easy to understand, spell, recognize, pronounce, and write.
3. Support product features and benefits.
4. Be adaptable to advertisements of different sizes, to packaging, and to other products in a line.
5. Avoid unpleasant or offensive connotations.

Selecting a name for its pleasing connotations is a common technique. Dove soap conveys the idea of something pure, white, soft, and gentle—attributes consumers look for in soap. Clairol's Quiet Touch™ does the same for a color rinse. A name may convey prestige. Many American cigarettes have names that sound British, which means prestige to many people in the United States: Marlboro, Pall Mall, Barclay, Kent. Some names state the actual product benefit. General Foods' Hamburger Helper™ is added to ground beef to make a variety of quick main dishes. Another strategy is to choose a word that sounds forceful, then apply that meaning to the product. "Shout," for instance, could be any of a number of products. "Want a tough stain out? Shout it out!" communicates the idea of a powerful laundry detergent.

Choosing an appropriate brand name is not easy, but the results for the right name are worth the effort. The name carries a message everywhere it goes. The stronger the message, the clearer the communication.

Discussion

1. Discuss the theory of supply and demand. Use the words "decrease," "increase," "price," "competition," "profits," and "production."

2. In what situations are the principles of supply and demand less valid? Why?

3. Manufacturers may have to generate demand. What causes this situation? What has it led to?

4. Explain the term "monopolistic competition." What effect does it have on prices?

5. Find advertising that emphasizes product uniqueness (monopoly).

6. Explain symbolic pricing. How does it work?

7. How can a low price slow demand? How can a high price increase demand?

8. Give examples of the product itself as the package.

9. What was the original purpose of a package? What are some of its other purposes today?

10. How can a package be a promotional tool? How can it be a form of marketing communication?

11. What are the three groups of requirements to consider in creating a package? What are the major requirements of each group?

12. Give further examples of convenience packaging.

13. What can a package do besides satisfy functional requirements? How?

14. Choose a package that you think has an effective design. Explain the reasons for your choice.

15. Choose additional packages and discuss how the material, shape, and size carry messages.

16. Find and discuss examples of merchandising on packages.

17. Why is the L'eggs package so effective?

18. Avon packages are also mentioned as outstanding. Why?

19. Give examples of both good and bad packaging used in your country.

20. Why is a brand name so important? Why did Standard Oil want a name with no meaning? What problem did they want to avoid?

21. Explain *brand, brand name,* and *brand mark.* Give examples of each.

22. List some prominent trade names in your country. Do you have trademarks? Are they protected by law? How is this demonstrated?

23. Give examples of these naming strategies for your country.
    a. company name plus product identification
    b. company name plus brand name
    c. brand name plus product identification
    d. brand name only

24. What are the characteristics of an effective brand name, according to the text? Are they the same in your country? If not, how do they differ?

25. Add brand names from your country to these examples.
    a. Dove and Quiet Touch™ (appropriate connotations)
    b. Pall Mall, etc. (prestige)
    c. Hamburger Helper™ (product benefit)
    d. Shout (forceful word)

Review

Mark T (True) or F (False) for each statement, according to the information in the text.

_____ 1. The only importance of price is its relation to supply and demand.

_____ 2. When price decreases, demand increases.

_____ 3. When price increases, profitability and production increase.

_____ 4. In good economic times and in affluent industrial societies, there is always a surplus of many products.

_____ 5. In monopolistic competition, every producer has a monopoly.

_____ 6. Pricing can be symbolic.

_____ 7. Consumers believe that "You get what you pay for."

_____ 8. Studies show a definite correlation between price and quality.

_____ 9. The only purpose of a package is to store and protect its contents.

_____ 10. For consumers, the major packaging requirement is convenience.

_____ 11. Convenience is a functional consideration for good packaging.

_____ 12. Package material, shape, and size help to communicate the product concept.

_____ 13. Soft, rounded shapes connote masculinity.

_____ 14. Packaging can be a means of merchandising.

_____ 15. Standard Oil Company of New Jersey wanted a name with an appropriate meaning.

_____ 16. A brand name can be spoken.

_____ 17. Xerox is a trademark.

_____ 18. Using a company name with a brand name is a brand-extension strategy.

_____ 19. Brand-extension strategies work best for well-established companies.

_____ 20. "Dove" is an appropriate name for a soap.

Objectives and Strategies

Special Terms

Objective
Aim or goal; what one wishes to accomplish.

Strategy
Plan; the means of reaching a goal.

Copy
The words written for a print advertisement or broadcast commercial.

Unit sales
Product sales, expressed in whole numbers.

Fiscal year
The financial year of a company. It is usually different from the calendar year. Example: September 1 to August 31.

Target market
The consumers toward whom advertising is directed; the segment of the population most likely to use the product.

DAGMAR
Defining Advertising Goals for Measured Advertising Results. Russell Colley's theoretical framework for setting advertising objectives.

Target audience
The people toward whom the advertising message is directed; those expected to see or hear it.

Survey
Means of questioning consumers about their attitudes and opinions, usually in person.

Questionnaire
 A survey in writing.
Hierarchy of effects
 Steps in a consumer's mental process before purchase based on the effects of advertising.
AIDA
 A hierarchy of effects of good advertising: Attention, Interest, Desire, Action.
USP
 Unique Selling Proposition. A product feature (benefit) around which an advertising campaign is constructed.
Execution
 The form that advertising takes.
Value-added theory
 Martin Mayer's theory that advertising itself adds value to a product.
Slogan
 A unique phrase identified with a company or brand.

Vocabulary Practice

1. What is another word for *objective?*

2. Define *strategy.* What is the relationship between an objective and a strategy?

3. What is *copy?*

4. How are *unit sales* expressed?

5. What is a *fiscal year?*

6. How does *target market* get its name?

7. What does *DAGMAR* stand for? Who originated the theory? What is its purpose?

8. How does a *target audience* differ from a target market?

9. What is a consumer *survey?*

10. What is the difference between a survey and a *questionnaire?*

11. Explain *hierarchy of effects.*

12. AIDA is an acronym. For what?

13. What does *USP* mean?

14. What is *execution?*

15. Who originated the *value-added theory?* Explain the theory.

16. What is a *slogan?*

Objectives and Strategies

The foundation of an effective advertising campaign is a sound advertising plan. The plan includes three groups of *objectives* and *strategies:* those for marketing, advertising, and *copy.* Each group is narrower and more specific in scope than the one before. Each helps to determine the next. The three are interrelated and interdependent.

Marketing objectives and strategies

Marketing objectives can be either short-term (one year) or long-term (three to five years). They should be expressed quantitatively, so as to be measurable; for example, "To increase *unit sales* from this year's 9,500,000 to 10,000,000 in the next *fiscal year,*" or "To increase our brand share by 10% during the next five years." Marketing strategies follow, spelling out a plan to reach the stated goals. Possible strategies include increasing the sales force, changing the product, and increasing advertising. Marketing strategies might mention advertising, but they do not tell, for instance, how advertising will be increased. That comes later, under advertising strategies.

Advertising objectives

Advertising is communication, so advertising objectives are expressed as communication goals. They are also measurable, and limited to a certain length of time, usually one year. An example of an advertising objective is, "If they are asked to name every brand they can think of in the product category, 40% of consumers in the *target market* will name our brand. This can be checked by survey one year after our advertising campaign has begun." Notice that the objective is not stated in terms of sales. Traditionally, sales have been the only measurement of advertising effectiveness. But in recent years, marketers have realized that sales are a result of many factors, not of advertising alone. The emphasis has therefore shifted to communication goals, quantifiably expressed.

This shift is due largely to the work of Russell Colley, who provided a theoretical framework for setting advertising objectives. In the early 1960's, Colley developed his *DAGMAR* approach (Defining Advertising Goals for Measured Advertising Results). Colley said that the only function of advertising was to communicate to a *target audience.* It should communicate information about the company and the product. It should create an attitude—readiness to buy the product—that would lead to purchase. Colley used six principles in his approach to advertising goals.

1. Advertising goals state the communication components of the total marketing effort.
2. They are stated in writing, in measurable terms.
3. Both planners and creative people (copywriters, designers) agree upon them. They agree on the nature of the message and of the target audience before they agree on exactly how to deliver the message.
4. They are based on real problems and opportunities. These are discovered by careful research, not by intuition or guess.
5. They establish a basis for later evaluation. For instance, consumer awareness of the brand is tested both before and after the advertising campaign.
6. At the same time they are stated, the specific means of later evaluation are also stated *(survey, questionnaire,* redemption of coupons, etc.).

The final goal of all advertising is to have consumers use the goods or the service. Russell Colley's model for attaining that goal names three stages that precede action. First is awareness that the product exists. Second is understanding of what the product is and what benefits it offers. Third is the decision to use the product. Then comes the actual purchase of the product or use the service.

This is a model of the *"hierarchy of effects."* These are steps that a consumer takes toward purchase. They also delineate the effects of advertising at the various stages.

In 1961, Robert J. Lavidge and Gary A. Steiner refined Colley's model. In their theoretical model, they named five steps in the movement toward purchase. They also outlined how the emphasis of advertising changes to expedite the process. They said that a consumer moves from awareness to knowledge, then liking. During this time, advertising gives factual information. Next the consumer reaches the level of preference, then conviction. At this point, consumers prefer the brand over all others, they want to buy it, and they are convinced that the purchase would be a wise one. Advertising in this period aims to change feelings and attitudes. It appeals to the emotions. As the consumer draws closer to purchase, advertising is directed at motives. It seeks to stimulate action.

A third model of the hierarchy of effects is *AIDA.* Like DAGMAR,

AIDA is an acronym. It stands for Attention, Interest, Desire, and Action. This familiar formula suggests that one good advertisement can move consumers through all four steps. First, it captures the attention; something in it catches the eye or the ear. Then there must be something that holds the interest of the reader, watcher, or listener. The advertisement should stimulate the consumer's desire to have the product. Finally, it should stir him or her to action.

The buyer behavior model uses the language of computers to summarize the decision process. It begins with recognition by the consumer of an unsatisfied need. The need motivates action, the search for ways to satisfy that need. The search narrows to a specific product. The consumer is aware of its existence, but lacks—and looks for—information about it. Next, he or she evaluates the information and considers the risks of purchase. "Will this product satisfy my need? Will it be worth the cost in time and money? What if I make the wrong decision?" At this point, the consumer decides whether to buy the product. If the consumer buys it, he or she decides whether he or she is satisfied or dissatisfied with it. If dissatisfied, the consumer begins the search again. If satisfied, he or she may decide to use it regularly.

Advertising strategies

All four models illustrate a process, that which happens in the minds of consumers as they move toward purchase. The models provide a theoretical foundation for establishing advertising objectives. In the advertising plan, these lead to advertising strategy. Objectives always tell what will be done, and strategy tells how. The advertising strategy is the main idea of the message that goes to consumers.

Probably the most prominent advertising strategy is the Unique Selling Proposition *(USP)*. The USP may be the unique product feature or benefit already discussed in Unit 3. But although there are truly unique products such as Crest toothpaste, they are rare. Today's market is highly competitive. Products in the same category are likely to be very similar. In order to sell the product, it may be necessary to "create" a difference. This does not mean to invent one where none exists. To do so may be against the law. Besides, consumers will quickly discover dishonesty in advertising, and sales will stop.

To "create" a difference, or a benefit, simply means to capitalize on a feature that will sell the product. Like all breweries, Schlitz washed its bottles with live steam—but consumers didn't know that the process was common. So the statement "Our bottles are washed by live steam" sold Schlitz beer. Discovering the USP is a matter of discovering the product's consumer strength. Research should reveal why people like a particular brand, or what they look for in that product category. Then advertising can be built around that idea. Advertising built around the USP must show benefit to the consumer. It should make a promise:

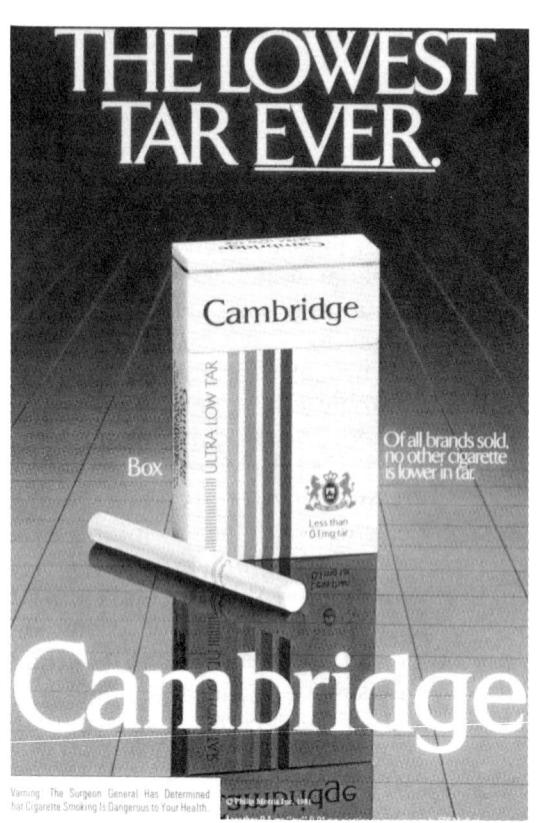

Hollow promise.

Our promise starts with the hollow tip at the end of our cigarette.

It keeps your lips from touching the tar that builds up on the filter. Flush filters can't do that.

Which is why Parliament Lights are so tastefully light.

And doesn't that sound promising?

Available in Soft Pack, Box and KKs.

© Philip Morris Inc. 1981

Only Parliament Lights has the famous recessed filter.

Soft Pack: 9 mg "tar," 0.7 mg nicotine—Box: 10 mg "tar," 0.7 mg nicotine—100's: 12 mg "tar," 0.9 mg nicotine av. per cigarette, FTC Report Dec.'

…edges & Me

Because the pleasure lasts longer.

…enson & Hedges Lights

"Here is what makes our product special, and here is how it will help you." It should also be a benefit that competitors cannot offer, or that they have failed to advertise. And it must be a very strong, persuasive idea.

The USP is not the only possible advertising strategy. Some advertisers use motivation as a strategy. They look for the "real reasons," conscious or unconscious, that consumers buy certain products. Others stress image. Still others believe it is the form of the advertisement itself, its *execution,* that provides the best strategy. In his book, *Madison Avenue U.S.A.,* Martin Mayer proposed his *value-added theory.* It is consistent with all of these strategies. Mayer said that advertising doesn't just inform and persuade. Advertising itself adds value to the product. Mayer saw that a new package or a new brand name changed the product in consumers' view. Advertising, he said, did the same. Whether the advertising strategy is based on USP, motivation, image, or execution, it translates the product concept into a consumer benefit. It supports the advertising objective of turning potential consumers into actual purchasers.

Advertising objectives and strategies define what will be done by advertising, and how. Their foundation is in research. Market research tells what competitors are doing. Along with product research, it leads to the discovery of product features and benefits. Consumer research underlies the models of the hierarchy of effects and the value-added theory. Effective advertising depends on thorough research. It also depends on the creative aspect—the visible part—of advertising.

Copy objective and strategy

Along with marketing and advertising objectives, the advertising plan contains the copy objective, also known as the creative objective. It focuses upon a copy problem: "Given our low brand awareness, how can our product best be positioned against the competition and in consumers' minds?" "Find the USP," or "Change the brand image," or "Think of a new name" won't answer the question. Those are advertising strategies, not solutions. They don't supply the words or the pictures or the music that will solve the problem. What is needed is the "big idea."

The big idea gives the product concept in capsule form. It ties together all of the elements in an advertising campaign. It is often summarized in a *slogan.* Slogans need to say something about product uniqueness or value. They should command attention, be memorable, and be brief. Slogans frequently use a play on words. These are examples of memorable (and sales-producing) slogans from United States advertising history.

Avis rental cars, which were well behind first-place Hertz: "We try harder."

SAVE A LETTUCE'S LIFE.

THIS LETTUCE STAYED FRESH FOR 15 DAYS IN THE GE FOOD SAVER. It's easy to keep lettuce this fresh and green for that long in a General Electric Food Saver refrigerator. Because its Moist 'n Fresh drawer lets you keep foods at the right temperature and humidity.

So leafy vegetables and your other moisture-loving foods thrive in it.

Fruits keep fresh for 15 days, too. Grapes, strawberries, oranges, all keep better in the lower humidity of our Cool 'n Fresh drawer.

Even meat and cheese stay fresh for 15 days. Because the sealed, high-humidity Snack Pack adds extra life to your unwrapped cold cuts and other uncovered snacks.

We can't think of a better feature than keeping your food fresh so long. (After all, that's what you buy a refrigerator for!) But, there's even more! Our Food Saver has adjustable glass shelves, an energy-saver switch—and it comes in a selection of sizes and styles; all are equipped for an automatic icemaker.

So, don't be a food waster. Get a GE Food Saver.

MODEL TBF-17Z

Unretouched photos were taken of lettuce and other food stored in Food Saver drawers after 15-day test.

WE BRING GOOD THINGS TO LIFE.

GENERAL ⊛ ELECTRIC

Clairol hair coloring: "Does she or doesn't she? (Only her hair-dresser knows for sure.)"
Bell (telephone) System: "Reach out and touch someone."
Maxwell House coffee: "Good to the last drop."
Morton salt: "When it rains, it pours."
Greyhound bus: "Leave the driving to us."

Creative professionals—and the public—seem to recognize the big idea when they see or hear it. It seems right. It appears to be very simple; the usual reaction is, "Why didn't I think of that?" The big idea is generally the result of working through hundreds of lesser ideas, of brainstorming and testing. This, again, is where all of the early research pays off. Information supports analysis, and analysis supports ideas. Still, all of the available methods of scientific research cannot replace creative observation. Marketing communicators need to use their own experience, too. They need to handle the product, talk to consumers, and study competitors' advertisements themselves. Creative people describe the creative process in various ways. In the end, though, big ideas spring from an indefinable inspiration.

Inspiration must be checked, however. To be successful, an idea has to be practical for execution. Copy strategy should clearly tell what the product is and how it is used. It should describe what the product does, and how that benefits consumers. An excellent copy strategy positions the product clearly in consumers' minds. Finally, it illuminates the character of the product, which will be reflected in the atmosphere and tone of the advertising.

Discussion

1. What are the three groups of objectives and strategies in an advertising plan? What is the relationship among the three groups? What is the difference between an objective and a strategy?

2. The advertising plan usually contains two kinds of marketing objectives. What are they? How should they be expressed?

3. Give additional examples of marketing strategies.

4. How are advertising objectives expressed? Why?

5. Why are sales no longer the only measurement of advertising effectiveness? What other factors besides advertising do you consider responsible for decreasing sales?

6. Whose work was instrumental in the shift to communication goals? What was his contribution?

7. What did he say advertising should do?

8. Briefly enumerate the six principles underlying advertising goals.

9. Name, in order, the steps in Colley's hierarchy of effects model.

10. Name the five steps in Lavidge and Steiner's model.

11. Go through the five steps and describe how the emphasis of advertising changes during the process.

12. How are the two models different? How are they similar?

13. Name and describe the four steps in AIDA.

14. Why is the language of computers used for the buyer behavior model?

15. How does that model differ from Colley's and from Lavidge and Steiner's?

16. How can purchase be a risk? What may result from the consumer's satisfaction with the product? His dissatisfaction?

17. Explain advertising strategy.

18. Find examples of USP's in advertising.

19. What can a marketing communicator do if there is no USP?

20. Study the respective benefit claims that are made for several products in a single product category; for example, several brands of cigarettes. Which claims are not truly unique but can apply to other brands in the same category?

21. Name three other advertising strategies.

22. Elaborate on the value-added theory. How is it consistent with the theories behind USP, motivation, image, and execution as advertising strategies?

23. Why does an advertising plan contain a copy objective?

24. Explain the big idea. What is it? Where does it come from? How do people recognize it? What restrictions are there on its use?

25. List slogans that have been successful in your country. Why do you think they have worked?

Review

Fill in the blanks with appropriate words from the text.

1. Objectives tell what will be done. _____ tell how objectives will be reached.

2. "By increasing advertising" is an example of a marketing _____.

3. Traditionally, _____ have been the only measurement of advertising effectiveness.

4. Advertising objectives are now expressed as _____ goals.

5. Russell Colley developed his _____ approach in the early 1960's.

6. He said that the only function of advertising was to communicate with a _____ _____.

7. Colley said that advertising objectives should be stated in writing, in _____ terms.

8. He set up a model of the hierarchy of _____.

9. His model has three steps that precede action: awareness, understanding and _____.

10. Lavidge and Steiner's model has five steps. They said that a consumer moves from awareness to knowledge, then _____.

11. Next comes preference, and finally, _____.

12. Advertising in this period appeals to the _____.

13. AIDA stands for _____, Interest, Desire, and _____.

14. Consumer _____ motivates action.

15. According to the buyer behavior model, _____ with a product may lead to adoption or non-adoption.

16. Probably the most prominent advertising strategy is the _____ _____ _____.

17. Products in the same category are likely to be very similar. In order to sell a product, it may be necessary to "_____" a difference.

18. Martin Mayer's theory is called the _____ theory.

19. The _____ objective is also called the creative objective.

20. "Leave the driving to us" is an example of a _____.

Media Planning

Special Terms

Medium
Any means by which an advertising message reaches consumers. Plural, *media.*

Point-of-purchase advertising
Advertising, such as shelf and counter displays, in places where consumers buy products; usually abbreviated POP.

Media mix
Manipulation of media variables in order to find the most effective and efficient combination.

Reach
The percentage of a target audience that is exposed to an advertising message at least once during a given time period.

Ratings
A measurement of reach or audience size. In television, one rating point is 1% of television households in the area covered.

Audience share
Another measurement of reach. A percentage of HUT during a given time.

HUT
Homes Using Television. A percentage, less than 100, of the households that have television.

GRP's
Gross Rating Points. The sum of all ratings for all advertising on or in all media during a given time frame.

Frequency
How many times an audience is exposed to a message in a certain time period.

Average frequency
> Mean frequency; number of message exposures in the average household.

Frequency distribution
> Breakdown of frequency figures by range; for example, "20% of television households had 2-4 exposures."

Continuity
> The timing of messages during a marketing period. If regularly timed throughout the period, continuity is high.

Wave theory
> A theory of media use that trades continuity for higher reach and frequency.

Reach theory
> A theory of media use that trades frequency and continuity for higher reach.

Media concentration theory
> A theory of media use that trades reach for higher frequency and continuity.

Media dominance theory
> A theory of media use that combines reach, frequency, and continuity.

CPM
> Cost per thousand. Measurement of media cost efficiency.

Vocabulary Practice

1. What is the singular form of *media?* Define it.

2. What is *POP?* Give an example.

3. What is the purpose of the *media mix?*

4. Explain *reach.* What are two ways of measuring it?

5. Define a television *rating point.*

6. Define *audience share.*

7. What is the difference between television households and *HUT?*

8. What are *GRP's?* What do they measure?

9. Define *frequency.*

10. Distinguish between *average frequency* and *frequency distribution.*

11. How is high *continuity* achieved?

12. What is the goal of advertisers who use the *wave theory?* Use the terms *reach, frequency,* and *continuity* in your answer.

13. Do the same for *reach theory, media concentration theory,* and *media dominance theory.*

14. What does *CPM* measure? What does it mean?

Media Planning

The execution of an advertising idea depends upon the *medium* that will be used. The major media are magazines and newspapers (print media) and radio and television (broadcast media). Minor media include outdoor advertising, *point-of-purchase advertising,* and direct mail. The *media mix* is a manipulation of these variables: which media will be used, how, and to what extent. The media planner's task is to match the product concept and its market requirements with appropriate media, so that the right message will reach consumers in the most effective and efficient way. There is no formula for the ideal media mix. The mix selected depends on a number of factors.

The first consideration might be how much money is available for advertising and merchandising. While television, for example, might be ideal for the message, TV advertising is very expensive. The cost may be prohibitive. Another consideration is the product's stage in the life cycle. The aim of advertising in the introductory stage is brand recognition. Wide media coverage, though expensive, may be necessary at that point. Price of the product influences the media mix. New products are often introduced at a premium price, in the hope of quickly recovering the expenses of introducing them. When the price is high, prestige is part of the product concept. The use of more prestigious media supports the message. Market segmentation is another important factor. Based upon demographic, psychographic, or geographic data, an effective media effort concentrates on the target market. Some media are more appropriate than others for certain products. Quality magazines, for example, are best suited to expressing the concept of a grand piano. Mass circulation magazines are better suited for products of general use. A final consideration is distribution. If the product is not distributed in a certain part of the country, there may be no point in advertising there. On the other hand, the product may be advertised there to encourage new distributors.

Reach

Several tools are available to the media planner. These include reach, frequency, and continuity. *Reach* is the percentage of a target audience that is exposed to an advertising message at least once during a certain time period, usually four weeks. "Exposed" doesn't mean that the message was actually seen or heard, only that the opportunity was present.

Ratings and shares measure reach. Ratings, or rating points, symbolize the size of the audience. They are used in the broadcast media, and increasingly in outdoor advertising. In television, one rating point equals 1%. The percentage is established by comparing television households reached with the total number of television households in the area. Imagine a city named Middletown, which has 200,000 television households. There, one rating point would equal 2,000 households (200,000 X .01). No station or program ever reaches a 100% rating; not all television sets are turned on at any one time.

Audience share is a percentage of all Homes Using Television *(HUT)* during a given time period. The total HUT figure for the period might be 70%. That is, 70% of all sets are on at the given time. For Middletown, the HUT figure would be 140,000. That figure is divided among the stations or programs in the area, according to number of viewers. For example, one station draws 84,000 households (a 60% share), the other 56,000 (a 40% share).

Gross Rating Points *(GRP's)* are the sum of all ratings for all advertisements in or on all media during a certain time period, usually a week or a month. Again, one rating point equals one percent of the audience reached. 450 GRP's equal 450%; an average frequency of 4.5 exposures to the message. GRP's are also equal to the product of reach times frequency.

Frequency

Frequency is the number of times a message reaches its audience during the four-week period. It can be expressed in two ways, average frequency and frequency distribution. *Average frequency* shows the average number of times the message reaches all members of the audience. Some will receive it more often, some less. *Frequency distribution* breaks down the audience by percentage for number of exposures.

Suppose a company buys a television spot in Middletown. The reach might be 80%; approximately 80% of the households were exposed to the message at least once during the four weeks. Average frequency might be 4.5; the average household was exposed to the message four and one-half times. Frequency distribution figures might show that 15% of the homes had 0-2 exposures, 25% had 3-5 exposures, and so on. Television is used here as an example. The same terms apply to other media as well.

It can be extremely expensive to try to achieve both high reach and high frequency. As new prospects are exposed, reach climbs. But then frequency has to increase, to keep pace with all of the new prospects. Therefore, media planners usually have to compromise. They more often emphasize reach for introducing new products. They sacrifice frequency in order to reach as many target consumers as possible. Their theory is that it is better to have the whole target market receive the message only twice, for example, than to have half of it receive the message six or eight times. Advertisers generally choose frequency over reach when advertising products that are purchased often, such as paper products. Competitors' activity influences this choice. With several brands of paper towels on the market, each wants to keep its name in people's minds for the regular shopping list.

Continuity

Continuity refers to the timing of messages. High continuity is continual advertising during a given marketing period, such as one year. Low continuity is occasional advertising during the same period. Often, continuity is traded for reach and frequency, especially during peak buying seasons. Many products have their own selling cycle. In the United States, more perfume, liquor, and hardcover books are sold in the four weeks before Christmas than during all the rest of the year. In the northern United States, more soft drinks are consumed in the summer than in the other seasons. Their manufacturers commonly advertise there throughout the year, but very heavily during July and August, and lightly in the other months. In the Southwest, where temperatures are warmer all year, there is a higher degree of continuity in soft drink advertising throughout the year.

Theories of media use

Striving for high reach, frequency, and continuity is, of course, also difficult and expensive. Again, compromises are made. They are based on the product's advertising needs and on the market situation. Four theories lend a framework for such compromises. The *wave theory* trades continuity for higher reach and frequency. The company advertises in selected media for comparatively short times throughout the year; for instance, four weeks at a time four times a year. It hopes for a carry-over effect from those times to the empty periods. The *reach theory* emphasizes reach at the expense of frequency and continuity. For example, an advertiser might buy space in a wide variety of magazines, all at the same time. In a *media concentration* approach, the advertiser focuses on a single medium. The company might buy a full page in every issue of one popular monthly magazine. This approach sacrifices reach for frequency and continuity. The *media dominance theory* combines all three media tools. An advertiser concentrates on one medium at a time, dominating it for a while. Then the effort moves to another medium for a short time. In this way, the advertiser has frequency in several media, but at different times; reach, through a variety of media for a longer time; and continuity, by using the different media in succession.

Cost

Another major concern in media planning is cost. Cost efficiency is measured by cost per thousand *(CPM)* target audience exposures. The formula for CPM is to multiply the cost of a message (rate) by 1,000 and divide the result by the number of people exposed to the message:

$$\frac{\text{rate x 1,000}}{\text{number exposed}} = \text{CPM}$$

An apparently small difference in CPM can mean a great difference in total cost. Suppose a target audience of 10,000,000 people. Media planning calls for an average frequency of one exposure per week, for four weeks, thirteen times a year. Total exposures are 520,000,000 (10,000,000 X 4 X 13). At a CPM of $11, the total cost would be $5,720,000. At a CPM of $12, the total cost would be $6,240,000. A CPM of one dollar less means a savings of $520,000.

There are other ways to reduce the media costs of an advertising campaign. Both print and broadcast media generally offer discounts to heavy users. Newspapers may have run-of-paper (ROP) programs. Radio and television stations may have run-of-station (ROS) programs. The newspaper or station gives reduced rates, but it decides when or where to run the advertisement. Some media offer special seasonal prices. In the United States, television viewing drops 20-30% in the summer. The same minutes that costs $1500 in May and June could cost more than twice as much in October, November, and December. Many magazines, and some newspapers, offer geographic editions. A hotel chain, for example, might advertise its hotels selectively in different editions.

QUIET
QUALITY

THE TIDES INN
Irvington, VA 22480
804/438-5000

The Classic Resort.

The MOUNT WASHINGTON
Box 1 Bretton Woods, N.H. 03575
Call toll free (in the N.E.) 1-800-258-0330 In N.H. 603-278-1000

Media objectives and strategies

All of these variables—price and distribution; the tools of reach, frequency, and continuity; the four theories of media use; and cost efficiency—are considered in establishing media objectives and strategies. Objectives and strategies should be clearly written and use measurable terms where possible.

Example media objectives are:

1. Focus advertising on new users.
2. Motivate reuse of the product.
3. Reach a market share of 8% by the end of the fiscal year.

Example media strategies are:

1. Direct the effort at young adults, ages 18-25.
2. Achieve a reach of 70 and an average monthly frequency of 6 among those young adults in key areas.
3. Continue the level of support after meeting those goals.
4. Use media that reflect the product concept, brand image, and copy requirements.

Specific plans for carrying out the objectives and strategies should follow; for example, exactly how money will be allocated to the various media.

The media planner faces a gigantic task. Today's consumer-oriented company might advertise in twenty different media. Determining the relative cost efficiency alone may be a job for a computer, not for a human being. The planner works with a great number of variables, too. Mountains of relevant data are available to be analyzed. Still, there is no substitute for personal interest and observation. Just as an advertiser needs to study the product and the consumer at first hand, the media planner has to study the media—in a personal way, putting himself in the place of the reader, the listener, or the viewer.

Discussion

1. What determines the type of execution an advertising idea will have? What are the major media?

2. Three examples of minor media are given. Can you think of others?

3. What is the principal object of media planning?

4. What factors does the selection of a media mix depend on?

5. Which media in your country are the more prestigious ones?

6. Give additional examples of how some media are more appropriate than others for certain products.

7. What are arguments for and against advertising in an area where a product isn't distributed?

8. How would rating points be used in outdoor advertising?

9. What does a television rating point equal? How is the percentage established?

10. Distinguish among ratings, audience share, and GRP's.

11. Distinguish among reach, frequency, and continuity.

12. Explain the significance of an average frequency of 12 in a four-week period.

13. Why is it so expensive to attempt to achieve both high reach and high frequency?

14. What are peak buying seasons in your country? Do you have a situation comparable to that before Christmas in the United States? Are there products such as soft drinks that have their own selling cycles?

15. Explain the wave theory in terms of reach, frequency, and continuity. Give an example of its application, from the text. Then, if possible, give an example that you have observed.

16. Do the same for the reach theory.

17. Do the same for the media concentration theory.

18. Do the same for the media dominance theory.

19. Give the CPM formula.

20. List three examples of general media objectives cited in the text.

21. What do ROP and ROS stand for? What do they mean?

22. What other possibilities for cutting media costs are mentioned in the text?

23. What possibilities are offered in your country?

24. Give further examples of media objectives.

25. Give further examples of media strategies.

Review

Mark T (True) or F (False) for each statement, according to the information in the text.

_____ 1. The execution of the essential advertising idea depends upon the medium to be used.

_____ 2. The principal broadcast media are radio and television.

_____ 3. POP is a major medium.

_____ 4. There is no formula for an ideal media mix.

_____ 5. Wide media coverage may be necessary to introduce a product.

_____ 6. There is no point in advertising where a product isn't distributed.

_____ 7. Reach is expressed as a percentage of a target audience exposed to an advertising message.

_____ 8. "Exposed" means that the message was seen or heard.

_____ 9. Television households and HUT are the same.

_____ 10. 500 GRP's=500%.

_____ 11. 5.0 is an expression of frequency distribution.

_____ 12. Attempting to achieve both high reach and high frequency is expensive.

_____ 13. Advertisers usually emphasize frequency when they introduce new products.

_____ 14. Continuity refers to the timing of messages.

_____ 15. Reach and frequency are more important than continuity during peak buying seasons.

_____ 16. The wave theory sacrifices reach for continuity and frequency.

_____ 17. The media concentration approach sacrifices frequency for reach and continuity.

_____ 18. The media dominance theory combines reach, frequency, and continuity.

_____ 19. The formula for CPM is $\frac{\text{rate x 1,000}}{\text{number exposed}}$.

_____ 20. "Focus advertising on new users" is an example of a media objective.

Special Terms

Print media
> Principally, newspapers and magazines.

Illustrations
> The photographs or drawings in a print advertisement.

Copy block
> Body copy or text of a print advertisement.

Headline
> Dominant words in a print advertisement. These are some types of headline, with their functions.

Benefit
>> Describes a product benefit.

Comparison
>> Compares the product to competitors' products.

How to
>> Tells how to use the product.

Command
>> Tells the reader what to do.

Question
>> Asks a question, often answered in the body copy.

Testimonial
>> Quotes a reference individual who uses the product.

Conversational
>> Quotes part of a dialogue or one person's words.

News
>> Uses words such as "now," "at last," and "new" to express novelty and immediacy.

Direct headline
> It contains the advertising message.

Indirect headline

It leads the reader to the text, where the advertising message is.

Logo

Logotype. The name or symbol of a company, store, or brand. Often a design, usually recognizable in print.

Subhead

Additional to the headline, but in smaller type.

Caption

Words in still smaller type that explain an illustration.

Vocabulary Practice

1. What are the principal *print media?*

2. What are *illustrations?*

3. What is the *copy block?*

4. Give the functions of these *headlines:*
   a. *Benefit*
   b. *Comparison*
   c. *How to*
   d. *Command*
   e. *Question*
   f. *Testimonial*
   g. *Conversational*
   h. *News*

5. What is the difference between a *direct headline* and an *indirect headline?*

6. Define *logo.*

7. What is the difference between a headline and a *subhead?*

8. What are *captions?*

Print Media

Print advertising deals with the use of space. A printed advertisement has four elements: illustration, headline, *copy block* (body copy or text), and logotype.

Illustrations

In a printed ad, the *illustration* usually dominates the space; most effectively, 60 to 70% of it. Studies show that one large illustration, with a single focus, is best. Next best is one large picture and two smaller ones. Effective illustrations vary in form and content, but most have several characteristics in common. They capture the attention of the target audience. They arouse interest in the product and often illustrate a product benefit. Good illustrations are relevant to the basic idea of the advertisement and to the words in headlines and body copy. They convey a tone or create an atmosphere and express feelings more directly and dramatically than words.

Photographs are by far more effective than any other illustration technique. They bring realism, immediacy, and often great beauty to the advertisement. Photographs have practical advantages as well. They are faster and less expensive to complete, and they are more adaptable to a variety of uses. In any technique, color is more effective than black and white. Tests of consumers' attention to and memory of advertising show this clearly. In women's magazines, the advantage of color over black and white is 68-70%; in newspapers, 45-70%. Although advertisements in color may cost 30% more, the expense is often justified by the results.

Color can be used for psychological motivation and effect. (This is also true in packaging.) The colors at one end of the spectrum—red, yellow, and orange—are warm, vibrant, stimulating. Green and blue are cool, relaxing colors. In the dominant culture of the United States, colors have symbolic meanings. Green is freshness, the outdoors, health. White is purity. Dark brown is masculine, and pastels are feminine. Black is sophisticated. Purple, deep red, and gold are regal and connote quality.

Illustration content varies widely, according to the product and the idea behind the advertisement. The illustration may show the product itself, the package, or the product in use. It often demonstrates a product benefit, such as the shine of a newly waxed floor, or the tough cleaning action of a washing machine. Illustrations of Armstrong products show beautifully decorated rooms that highlight Armstrong floor tiles and acoustical ceilings. The pictures show how they will look in a real setting. Comparison and competition are common themes. Diet products will show "before" and "after" pictures of people who used the product. Cold and headache remedies will be contrasted to competitors'. Cigarette manufacturers vie for the lowest tar ratings. Illustrations often depict the results of not using the product: dishes that aren't quite clean, the plight of the person who didn't buy the right kind of insurance. The illustration may tell a story or dramatize a situation. It may have no "content" at all, but it creates a relevant impression.

The Polaroid SX-70 Auto

With New Time-Zero Supercolor Film.

Together, the Polaroid SX-70 AutoFocus and Time-Zero Supercolor film represent a new dimension in instant photography. Together, they took on the Tucson Rodeo and returned with these bold, beautiful photographs.

1   Open, this gate releases 2,000 pounds of raging bull. Closed, it makes a stunning graphic. Great compositions like these are possible because unlike other instant cameras the SX-70 AutoFocus is an SLR. So, what you see through the lens is the picture you get.

2   Bright red feathers, a blue Arizona sky and a noble suntanned face. All are faithfully reproduced by the unique dyes in new Polaroid Time-Zero Supercolor film in this portrait of Geronimo III, grandson of the legendary Apache chief.

3   You almost want to reach into this picture and touch the Rios Brothers handtooled saddle. Unlike other instant cameras which have plastic lenses, the SX-70 AutoFocus has a four-element glass lens which can give you a clear, crisp image like this.

4   With the SX-70 AutoFocus, it was a lot easier to capture this picture than it was for champion Alan Laneville to rope that calf. While you just aim and shoot, the exclusive sonar AutoFocus system measures the distance to your subject and whips the lens into precise focus. Instantly and automatically.

5   Each single cord of this woven cinch strap is strikingly delineated in this intricate close-up. No other camera lets you move in this close-as close as 10.4 inches-without expensive extra lenses.

6   Each click of the shutter brings a unique sharing experience into focus for you and your subject. In just 10 seconds, the fun begins to develop. Just ask champion barrel riders Kelly Kay and Jan Hansen.

Wherever your imagination leads you, only the Polaroid SX-70 AutoFocus lets you leave with wonderful photographs like these right in your hands. Choose the SX-70 AutoFocus in familiar chrome and leather, or the new Model II in matte black with a pebble grained leather-look finish at a greatly reduced cost.

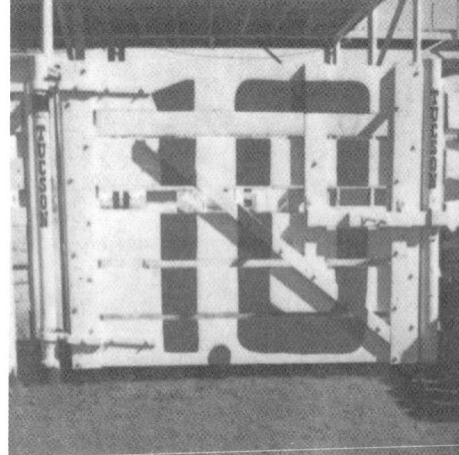

1

4

No other instant camera comes close.

Focus goes to the Rodeo.

3

6

Headlines

Headlines should draw attention; 80 to 90% of readers never read beyond them. If the headline fails to draw their interest immediately and forcefully, they won't read the text. The appearance of the headline alone is often the attention-getting device. By definition, it is printed in larger type than the rest of the advertisement. Headlines frequently use capital letters with small ones, italics, and other punctuation such as quotation, question, and exclamation marks. Headlines are usually short, one to six words on a single line, since a few words stand out in space better than many. Readers can easily grasp a few words at one glance. Brevity should not be more important than meaning, however. It may take more than six words, or more than two lines, to deliver the essential message to the right readers.

The ability to draw attention, brevity, and appeal to the target market are characteristics of good headlines. The headline should also say something about the product—brand name, slogan, or benefit, for example. The message should apply to the specific brand only, not to others in the same category. It should stimulate interest in reading further. For this reason, it must be closely related to the text, as well as to the illustration. A good headline is active in both form and content.

There are a number of techniques for writing headlines; all are valid, provided that they reinforce the basic idea of the advertisement. The *benefit* headline describes a product benefit. The *comparison* headline contrasts the company's brand and competitors' brands. *"How to"* headlines tell how to do something. Some issue *commands,* others ask *questions.* The question is a useful device for leading readers into the body copy, where the question is answered. Command headlines easily convert to "how to" headlines: "Do this" into "How to do this." *Testimonials* from reference individuals often appear in both headlines and illustrations. The conversational headline reports part of a dialogue or quotes an individual. Words such as "at last," "finally," "now," and "new" give *news* headlines their name. *Direct* headlines contain the advertising message; *indirect* headlines carry the reader to the text.

Body copy

According to research, the optimal amount of body copy uses less than 20% of the total advertising space. As with headlines, shorter is better, again provided that meaning is not sacrificed. The major function of headlines and illustrations is to attract attention and arouse curiosity. The major function of the body copy is to satisfy that curiosity. If the headline tells how to do something, the text amplifies the instructions. If the headline asks a question, the text answers it. If the illustration shows someone who failed to use the product, the copy tells how to correct the mistake. In general, the most effective copy tells buyers how to satisfy their needs and solve their problems. It does this in a clear, concise, and personal way. Finally, it suggests action: where to find the product and, often, its price.

There are no strict rules for writing outstanding advertising copy. Different people work successfully in different ways, with different styles and approaches. However, here are some useful suggestions that work in English and in the United States.

1. Use short sentences with short, familiar words.
2. Use positive forms or strong negatives. Strong negatives are "never," "avoid," and "stop." Avoid weak negatives such as "don't," "won't," and "can't." Emphasize the positive in grammar and in attitude.
3. Use contractions the way people use them when they talk. People do not (don't) use the full forms except in formal writing.
4. Use the active voice. "Floors clean better with _____" is stronger than "Floors can be cleaned better with _____."
5. Use the present tense. "My floor is cleaner with _____" is stronger than "I used _____, and my floor was cleaner."
6. Use only necessary words—as many or as few as needed to communicate the message.
7. Make the message personal; direct it at the consumer. Each consumer likes to believe that the message is for him individually.
8. Keep the essential idea in mind at all times. Eliminate even brilliant ideas that are irrelevant.
9. Feel enthusiasm for the product and let that excitement show in the copy. But be truthful and don't exaggerate.
10. Concentrate on the consumer and product benefits. Write from the reader's point of view. Write what the buyer wants to know.

Logo

The fourth major element of print advertising is the logotype, or *logo*. The logo is the name or symbol of a company, store, or brand. It is often a design, and it is usually recognizable in print. The distinctive lettering of Coca-Cola™ is both a brand mark and a logo. The logo often appears in the lower right-hand corner of an advertisement. The slogan and a picture of the package often accompany it. They use little space, usually no more than 5%.

Subheads and captions

Besides the four major elements, many advertisements also use subheads and captions. *Subheads* are in smaller type than headlines. If space is a problem for the headline, additional material can sometimes appear as subheads. They can also summarize that which the text elaborates, for example, by naming several product uses. *Captions* are sentences of one or two lines under or next to the illustration. They are in still smaller type. Captions explain the illustration.

Design

Design—the arrangement of elements on the page—is a concern of everyone who creates print advertising. This is because all of the elements have to work together, not only in content but in form. The arrangement depends on how space will be used for contrast; the size and number of illustrations; the sequence of several illustrations (vertical, horizontal, or blocks of both); and the logical relationships of the elements. Every good design has a single focus, usually the illustration or the headline. The focus gives the reader a starting point and leads him into the rest of the advertisement. The other elements should follow a natural flow. Readers of English are accustomed to going from top to bottom, and from left to right, on a page. Consequently, that is the most common arrangement for advertisements in the United States. Several devices will help readers follow the intended sequence: numbers, arrows, lines, and pointing hands, for example. Eyes follow eyes. Action should face into the advertisement, not away from it. Models' eyes should focus on the central element of the advertisement, so that readers will do the same; or look into readers' eyes, to enhance the personal appeal.

Newspapers vs. magazines

Most print advertising is designed for newspapers and magazines. The elements discussed in this unit apply equally to advertising for both. But which is the better media vehicle? Throughout this book, the emphasis is on national advertising of consumer goods. Few newspapers are truly national. The choice of one medium above the other depends first upon the location of the target audience. National advertising in newspapers is expensive, and it has to compete with local advertising. Apart from those considerations, newspapers have certain advantages over magazines. Usually within a narrow geographical range, they provide very high reach. They are more cost efficient on a CPM basis. Readers' interest in advertising is higher. Newspapers offer more options in size of space and time of appearance for ads.

On the other hand, magazines are printed on paper of higher quality, so print looks better and color reproduction is better. Advertising in magazines carries more prestige. Special interest magazines make it easier to reach a specific audience. People read newspapers quickly and throw them away; newspaper advertisements are short-lived. Magazines advertisements are long-lived. People take more time to read a magazine. They may look at it again and again, then give it to someone else.

In general, the choice of print medium depends upon such major factors as the product concept, advertising objectives, and the advertising budget.

Discussion

1. Name the four major elements of print advertising.

2. Why does the illustration usually dominate the space? Why is one large illustration better than several smaller ones?

3. List several common characteristics of good illustrations.

4. Why are photographs more effective than drawings?

5. What practical advantages do photographs offer?

6. Why is color more effective than black and white?

7. Do you agree that red, yellow, and orange are "warm, vibrant, stimulating"? That green and blue are "cool and relaxing"? If not, which colors would you describe in those ways?

8. Give symbolic meanings for colors in your culture. Which are similar to those in the United States? Which are different?

9. Which colors do you feel are appropriate for advertising which kinds of products?

10. Find an example of an advertisement that illustrates a product benefit.

11. Find an example of an advertisement that illustrates a comparison.

12. Find an example of an advertisement that illustrates "before" and "after."

13. Find an example of an advertisement that illustrates the results of not using the product.

14. Why is it necessary for a headline to draw attention? What are some ways it does this?

15. Why are headlines usually short?

16. List several characteristics of good headlines.

17. Find or write an example of each of these.
    a. a benefit headline
    b. a comparison headline
    c. a how to headline
    d. a command or question headline
    e. a testimonial headline
    f. a news headline

18. Find or write examples of direct and indirect headlines.

19. What are some characteristics of effective body copy?

20. Why, in English, do short sentences with short, familiar words make the most effective copy? Is this true in your language and culture?

21. Why is it suggested that printed copy should read the way people talk? Is this true in your language and culture?

22. Does your language have forms that correspond to contractions, active voice, and present tense? Are they also used in advertising?

23. Collect some familiar logos.

24. Find an advertisement that you think is well-designed. Analyze it, using the concepts in the text.

25. Name several comparative advantages and disadvantages of newspapers and magazines.

Review

Fill in the blanks with appropriate words from the text.

1. The copy block is also called the body copy or the _____.

2. In a print advertisement, the illustration dominates the _____.

3. A good illustration must capture the attention of the _____ _____.

4. _____ are more effective than any other technique of illustration.

5. Green and _____ are cool, relaxing colors.

6. An illustration of a shining newly waxed floor demonstrates a product _____.

7. The headline is printed in larger _____ than the rest of the advertisement.

8. Because of space, and for the convenience of readers, headlines are usually _____.

9. But brevity shouldn't be more important than _____.

10. A _____ headline contrasts the company's brand and competitors' brands.

11. _____ from reference individuals often appear in both headlines and illustrations.

12. _____ headlines contain the advertising message.

13. Copy should be written the way people _____.

14. The message should be _____, directed at the consumer.

15. The four major elements of print advertising are illustration, headline, copy block, and _____.

16. If space is a problem for the headline, sometimes material can be moved to _____.

17. _____ are sentences of one or two lines that explain illustrations.

18. The arrangement of elements on the page is the _____.

19. Most print advertising is for _____ and _____.

20. Advertising in _____ carries more prestige.

Broadcast Media

Special Terms

Broadcast media
Principally, radio and television.

Circulation
For newspapers and magazines, the numbers of copies sold. For radio or television, "circulation" is measured by exposure.

Coverage
The number of potential radio listeners or television viewers.

Local advertising
Space or time bought by a local, not a national, advertiser.

Spot
One unit of air time. National advertisers buy spots from local stations and networks.

Dayparts
Classification of broadcast periods.

Drive time
Morning and afternoon drive times are two of the radio dayparts. The name comes from the times when people are driving to and from work.

Avail
A time slot or availability purchased by a radio advertiser.

Jingle
A form of commercial in which a short rhyme is set to music.

Commercial
A broadcast advertisement.

Network
A connected system of radio or television stations.

Affiliate
A member of a network.

Sponsorship

A means for advertisers to buy television time. Sponsorship of a program means complete responsibility for production costs and for advertising on the program.

Participation

Another way to buy television time. Several advertisers cooperate to buy time on one or more programs.

Prime time

Period of the day when television viewing is highest: 7:30-11 p.m. in the United States.

Fringe

Period before (early fringe) and after (late fringe) prime time: 4:30-7:30 p.m. and 11 p.m.-1 a.m. in the United States.

Vocabulary Practice

1. What are the two principal *broadcast media?*

2. How do newspapers and magazines measure their *circulation?* How is "circulation" measured for radio and television?

3. What is *coverage?*

4. Who buys *local advertising?*

5. Who sells *spots?* What are they?

6. What are *dayparts?*

7. Does *drive time* apply to radio or to television? How many drive times are there each day? Where does the name come from?

8. *Avail* is a short form of what word?

9. What is a *jingle?*

10. What is a *commercial?*

11. What are *network affiliates?*

12. Explain television program *sponsorship.*

13. Explain television program *participation.*

14. Define *prime time.* When does it occur in the United States?

15. Define *fringe.* What time periods are early fringe and late fringe in the United States?

Broadcast Media

Time vs. space. That is the essential difference between the broadcast media and the print media. Newspapers and magazines exist in space. Their pages are tangible. Advertising in print media occupies space. Radio and television exist in time. Their broadcasts are intangible. Advertising on TV or radio occupies time. A consumer can pick up a newspaper, or more likely a magazine, and look at its messages again and again. Once a message is broadcast, it is gone forever. Another difference between the two types of media is a difference of purpose. The major function of print media is to provide news and information; of the broadcast media, to provide entertainment. The reach of newspapers and magazines is limited only by how far their publishers care to send them. The reach of radio and television is limited by the strength of station (channel) transmitters. The number of copies of a newspaper or magazine that go to consumers represents its *circulation*. A radio or TV station's number of potential listeners or viewers is its *coverage*. Its "circulation" is measured by exposure.

Radio

In the United States, radio began as an all-purpose medium. It offered news, editorials, information, and entertainment of many kinds. Beginning in the late 1920's, it offered commercial advertising. Early in the 1950's, television emerged as a rival medium. The added visual element made television immensely popular. For a while, it looked as though radio would be unable to survive. But, in time, radio responded aggressively. It became a specialized, rather than an all-purpose, medium. The emergence of FM stations aided specialization. FM stations have low, narrow frequencies and short range. There is room on the radio dial for many more FM stations than AM stations. An FM station therefore can appeal to a narrow, special-interest audience. This diversity is especially apparent in large metropolitan areas. At the same time, advertisers began to concentrate less on broad market appeal and more on market segmentation. Radio provided ready-made target markets. Radios became so inexpensive that virtually everyone could afford at least one. Radio is now the specialized medium that can be found almost everywhere in the world.

Since the advent of television, network radio advertising in the United States has decreased greatly. The emphasis is now on local and spot advertising. *Local advertising* is bought by a local advertiser. A *spot* is one unit of air time, usually one minute or less. National advertisers buy spots directly from individual local stations, much as they do advertising space in local newspapers. Radio spots in the United States are most expensive at 7:30 a.m., because that is when radio has the

The
Sixth
Van Cliburn
International
Piano
Competition

It's
intense
dramatic
and
inspiring

Sunday
May 31
7:30 pm EDT
PBS
check local
listings

Produced by
KERA-TV

Made
possible
by a
grant from
IBM

most listeners. As the day continues, listening diminishes gradually, except for an afternoon peak between 3 and 6 p.m.

Radio time is classified by *dayparts:* drive time, housewife time, weekend time, and evening time. There are two *drive times.* The morning drive (AMD) is 6-10 a.m., Monday through Friday. The afternoon drive is 3-7 p.m., Monday through Friday (PMD). The audience for both periods consists of people driving to and from work, preparing meals, and working; children not in school; and teenagers. Housewife time is 10 a.m. to 3 p.m., Monday-Friday (DAY, or daytime). Despite the name, the audience includes both men and women on the job outside the house. Weekend time is SAM and WKND. SAM is Saturday morning from 6 to 10 a.m.; WKND is weekend, 10 a.m. to 7 p.m. Saturday and 6 a.m.-7 p.m. Sunday. Evening is NIGHT, from 7 p.m. to midnight.

The time a radio advertiser purchases is a slot or availability *(avail).* Few buy only one. Rather, they buy a group of avails, in order to reach a mass audience. They set exposure goals, which are expressed in GRP's.

Many people buy magazines because they want to read advertisements. On radio, advertising interrupts. From the advertiser's point of view, this is both a strength and a weakness. The interruption itself can be an attention-getting device. It can prepare people to listen to the message. But the interruptions are also a source of irritation. They can cause people *not* to listen; in fact, to resent the advertisement and the advertiser. This dual effect of interruptions places a burden on anyone who writes advertising copy for radio. So do two other characteristics of the medium. First, it is purely aural; sound effects must do all of the work. Second, few people just sit and listen to the radio. Most are doing something else at the same time. The advertisement has to seize their attention immediately, preferably within eight seconds. Then the remaining content of the ad has to hold their attention.

Sound effects and music are attention-getters. Radio, after all, gave birth to the *jingle,* a rhyme set to music. The jingle approach is still a common type of radio *commercial.* In general, jingles are very effective in catching attention and maintaining audience interest. However, the rhyme and the music tend to obscure the message, and listeners tire of jingles quickly.

Another type of commercial is the narrative. The story is usually in the form of a humorous dialogue. Commercials are often celebrity testimonials. These are statements by reference individuals about the value of a specific brand. The celebrity claims personal use of the product and satisfaction with it.

Another form of commercial is the interview, either with a legitimate customer or, humorously, with a pretend one. Some commercials are aural presentations of product use and benefit. Sounds, such as coffee bubbling in a percolator or meat frying in a pan, can involve listeners' imaginations and support the product concept.

Whatever type of commercial is used, time places a severe limit on content. Radio commercials are normally ten, twenty, thirty, or sixty seconds long. On the average, only two words can be spoken each second. In writing a radio commercial it is best to focus on only one idea, largely because of the time limit.

Listeners expect radio to bring them news, information, and entertainment. Effective radio advertising is in harmony with their expectations. A new product or a special price can be news. The commercial can inform consumers about the product and its benefits. Through music, sound effects, and humor, advertising can entertain. Repetition of the brand name and the advertisement's basic idea helps listeners to remember them. Spoken words replace the visible words of print advertising. Words can help consumers to visualize the product and the package. As in print advertising, natural, conversational language works best.

Advantages of radio as an advertising medium are its cost, its specialized nature, and its flexibility. On a CPM basis, radio is the least expensive major medium. It can be very selective in reaching target markets. It is flexible geographically and in the variety of time slots it can offer.

Television

Television is probably the most potent of all advertising media. Unlike any other, it combines sight and sound. It shows real action, it is personal, and it is true to life. In many countries, the television audience is larger than that for any other form of mass communication.

In the United States, there are three major commercial television *networks.* Usually the networks require advertisers to buy time on a minimum number of station *affiliates.* In effect, this method provides national coverage, since the stations are scattered throughout the country. Network scheduling is one of the advertiser's geographical choices. The other is local scheduling. Rather than having one contract that covers many stations, the advertiser signs a separate contract with each local station. For advertisers who want national coverage, this is a less desirable method. Most national advertisers use network scheduling, perhaps supplementing it with local spots.

Spot announcements are one of the ways that advertisers can buy time. They are available only from local stations. They appear between programs, not within them. Since several spots often run consecutively, advertising clutter results, and spots receive little attention. The other ways to buy time are sponsorship and participation. *Sponsorship* means complete responsibility for production costs and for advertising on the program. Sponsorship is extremely expensive, but it offers advantages to the advertiser, such as control over the type of program to be sponsored. Sponsorship also gives opportunities for extensive merchandising and for commercials longer than sixty seconds. *Participation* is joining with other advertisers to buy commercial time on one or more programs. Participating advertisers have no financial responsibility for program production. Using participating spots on several programs extends reach and reduces frequency, while GRP's remain stable. CPM is usually much lower.

The timing of commercials is a major concern of television advertisers. Conversely to radio, television viewing gradually increases during the day. TV time, like radio time, is classified by dayparts. Monday-Friday (day) is 10 a.m. to 4:30 p.m. Saturday and Sunday (day) is 7 a.m. to 7:30 p.m. Early fringe is 4:30-7:30 p.m., bordering on *prime time,* which is 7:30 to 11 p.m. Late *fringe* follows, from 11 p.m. to 1 a.m. As the name suggests, prime time has the largest share of viewers—and the most expensive commercial time.

While television is not so selective as radio, TV advertisers do have a degree of selectivity. One tool is the time of day. For example, in the United States, the time to reach men is Saturday and Sunday afternoons; children, Saturday mornings; teenagers, the late fringe period on Friday and Saturday nights. A second tool is type of program. More men watch sports, more women watch dramas. Special programming such as sports championships and multi-episode dramas offers opportunities to advertisers. Such programming may supply a captive audience for several hours. Special programs of unusually high quality attract affluent, educated viewers and lend prestige to the sponsors or participating advertisers.

VHF (very high frequency) and UHF (ultra-high frequency) are the most familiar forms of television. They are transmitted through the air by radio waves and can be received on a limited number of channels. Cable TV is transmitted through the air and by wires. It allows the use of an almost unlimited number of channels. Cable TV, therefore, offers the possibility of much more specialized programming and increased selectivity for advertisers.

Guidelines for writing outstanding TV advertisements are similar to those for writing other types of ads. The television commercial also begins with an idea, which provides the focus. All elements of the commercial, both audio and visual, reinforce each other and relate to the basic idea. The marketing communicator who writes for television should capitalize on its visual aspects. The video carries the message, with the audio interpreting when necessary. Writers of television advertising should also take advantage of TV's ability to show action. Action holds viewers' attention and keeps the commercial moving forward.

Television lends itself to product demonstration better than any other medium. Demonstration is a popular "story-telling" technique on television commercials. Although the writer must think of commercials as idea-carrying messages, viewers feel that they are watching a story.

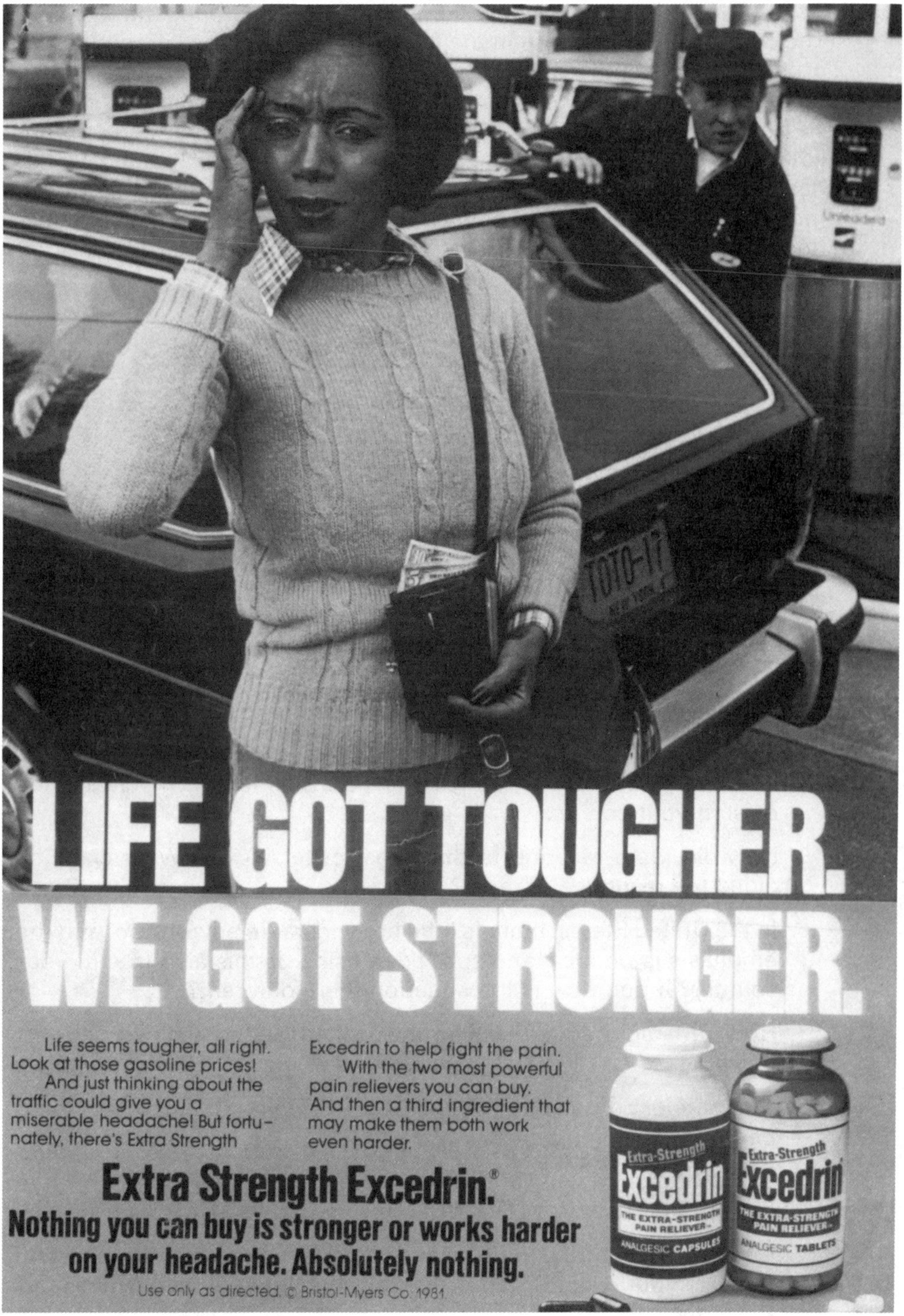

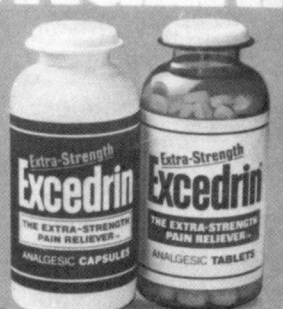

LIFE GOT TOUGHER.
WE GOT STRONGER.
Life seems tougher, all right. Look at those gasoline prices! And just thinking about the traffic could give you a miserable headache! But fortunately, there's Extra Strength Excedrin to help fight the pain.
With the two most powerful pain relievers you can buy. And then a third ingredient that may make them both work even harder.
Extra Strength Excedrin.®
Nothing you can buy is stronger or works harder on your headache. Absolutely nothing.
Use only as directed. © Bristol-Myers Co. 1981
Extra-Strength Excedrin THE EXTRA-STRENGTH PAIN RELIEVER ANALGESIC CAPSULES
Extra-Strength Excedrin THE EXTRA-STRENGTH PAIN RELIEVER ANALGESIC TABLETS

How to do something, or how something works, is one kind of story. The demonstration may be in the form of a solution or a comparison. A problem is presented at the beginning of the story—dirty clothes, a hungry child, a headache. Use of the product solves the problem. A comparison story shows the specific brand victorious over one or more competitive brands. The clothes are cleaner, the child is happier, the headache goes away faster. These forms are not only demonstrations, they are real dramas. They show people who look real, in familiar situations from real life. They involve the viewer (consumer), as all good advertising should.

Discussion

1. Discuss the implications of this fact: The essential difference between print and broadcast media is the difference between space and time.

2. What is the difference in purpose between the two groups of media?

3. Discuss the differences between the two groups in terms of reach, circulation, and coverage.

4. What other differences can you think of? Mention the media as they exist in your country.

5. How did radio respond to the threat of television? What changes aided the response of radio?

6. In the United States, there is little network radio advertising, and the emphasis is on local and spot advertising. Is this also true in your country? If not, how is the situation there different?

7. How can radio advertisers in the United States achieve national reach?

8. Compare or contrast the United States and your country regarding peak radio listening times.

9. Is radio time in your area classified by dayparts? If so, what are they? If not, how is it classified?

10. Compare or contrast the specific dayparts in the United States with those in your country. When are corresponding times? Who listens

during those times?
a. AMD
b. PMD
c. DAY
d. SAM
e. WKND
f. NIGHT

11. On radio, advertising interrupts. How is this fact both a strength and a weakness?

12. What other characteristics of radio place a burden on radio advertisers?

13. Do you have jingles on your local radio stations? If so, name some prominent ones.

14. What are advantages and disadvantages of jingles?

15. Name some other forms of radio advertising.

16. Time places a severe limit on the content of commercials. What are some implications of this fact?

17. How can radio advertising harmonize with consumers' expectations of the medium?

18. What are advantages of radio as an advertising medium?

19. What are advantages of television as an advertising medium?

20. How can a television advertiser in the United States approach having national coverage?

21. What are three ways to buy television time? Name, define, and explain each one.

22. Compare or contrast these aspects of television timing in the United States with timing in your country.
a. weekday
b. weekend
c. early fringe
d. prime time
e. late fringe

23. How can television advertisers in the United States achieve selectivity? How do these facts compare with the facts where you live?

24. Name and describe at least three kinds of demonstration "story" that television commercials might tell about a product. Give any examples that you have seen.

Review

Mark T (True) or F (False) for each statement, according to the information in the text.

_____ 1. The essential difference between print advertising and broadcast advertising is time vs. space.

_____ 2. The major function of print advertising is to entertain.

_____ 3. The reach of newspapers and magazines isn't limited by distance.

_____ 4. A radio or television station's "circulation" is its coverage.

_____ 5. FM stations increase radio's selectivity.

_____ 6. Radio is an all-purpose medium.

_____ 7. National advertisers can buy local advertising on radio.

_____ 8. As the day continues, the number of radio listeners in the United States increases.

_____ 9. Both men and women listen to the radio during housewife time.

_____ 10. Most radio advertisers buy a group of avails.

_____ 11. On radio, advertising interrupts.

_____ 12. Few people just sit and listen to the radio.

_____ 13. The jingle is a form of commercial, a rhyme set to music.

_____ 14. On the average, a person speaks about five words per second on radio.

_____ 15. Radio is the most expensive medium, on a CPM basis.

_____ 16. In television, participation means complete responsibility for program production costs.

_____ 17. Television viewing in the United States increases during the day.

_____ 18. Commercial time is most expensive during prime time.

_____ 19. Television is more selective than radio.

_____ 20. On television, the video carries the message, and the audio interprets it when necessary.

Merchandising

Special Terms

Sales promotion
> Concerted, short-term efforts aimed at encouraging sales. Merchandising, directed at three groups: the sales force, the trade, and the consumer.

Sales force
> A company's own salespeople.

Commission
> Extra payment to the sales force, for example, as a reward for sales. Usually a percentage of the sales.

Trade promotion
> Sales promotion directed to retailers.

Stocking allowance
> A method of trade promotion by which retailers are rewarded for buying the product.

Loading
> A form of stocking allowance in which retailers receive a commission for increasing their inventories.

Inventory
> The amount of a product that a retailer has in stock, either on shelves or in storage.

Leasing
> Another form of stocking allowance, in which a company rents a section of a retail store for a short time.

Free goods offer
> Also a form of stocking allowance. The retailer might, for example, receive one case of free goods for every five he or she buys.

PM
> Push Money. A commission to retail salespeople for personally encouraging consumers to buy a product.

Shelf-talker

A strip of paper along the front edge of a store's display shelf, which advertises the product behind it.

These are forms of consumer promotion:

Contest

A competition, based on skill, offering prizes.

Sweepstakes

A competition, based on luck, offering prizes.

Refund

The return of all or part of a purchase price.

Sample

A small amount of the product given to consumers to encourage them to buy the product.

Premium

A gift offered for using the product.

Price-off

A discount, usually in the form of a cents-off label or a two-for-the-price-of-one offer.

Coupon

A piece of paper distributed by a manufacturer or by a store. Upon redemption, it returns part of the purchase price to the buyer.

Cross-ruff

A coupon on one product's package that is valid toward the purchase of another, related product.

Self-destruct

A new form of coupon where one coupon is printed partly over another.

Vocabulary Practice

1. Define *sales promotion.* Name three groups toward which it is directed.

2. Who are the members of a *sales force?*

3. What is a *commission?* What is it usually based on?

4. Who are the *trade?*

5. What is a *stocking allowance?* Name three kinds.

6. What does *loading* mean?

7. What is a retailer's *inventory?*

8. Describe *leasing.*

9. Give an example of a *free goods offer.* To whom is it made?

10. Who receives *push money?* For what?

11. What is a *shelf-talker?* Where is it found?

12. Define these forms of consumer promotion.
    a. *Contest*
    b. *Sweepstakes*
    c. *Refund*
    d. *Sample*
    e. *Premium*
    f. *Price-off*
    g. *Coupon*

13. Name and describe two kinds of coupon.

Merchandising

Merchandising supplements advertising. It takes two broad forms— sales promotion and promotion through minor media.

Sales promotion

Advertising and *sales promotion* differ in several respects. A merchandising effort is usually of very short duration. Advertising generally continues over a much longer period. Advertising creates an attitude that may lead to sales. Merchandising gives added incentive to buy. It calls for immediate action. Merchandising always supplements advertising; it cannot replace it. Many consumers have become cynical about advertising and resistant to it. They see little difference between brands in a product category. Sales promotion provides a clear, attractive differentiation. It offers something beyond the advertised benefits of a product. Sales promotion has a specific, narrow objective.

Some experts say that merchandising is most effective for new products and for major changes in old ones. Others say that it works best when a product nears the end of its life cycle. Both views have research support, and both are logical. Because of its immediacy, sales promotion can bring vitality to a product at any stage. It cannot, however, reverse declining sales figures by itself. It cannnot change non-acceptance of a product to acceptance. Nor can sales promotion build brand loyalty. Brand loyalty comes about after a long period of many trials. Merchandising efforts are brief and seldom repeated.

Merchandising best serves to induce consumers to try a product. For sales over the long term, the product must then deliver the promised benefit. If the product does deliver its promise, merchandising can encourage people to try the product again. In this way, it can aid in establishing patterns of purchase. Sales promotion can often increase consumption of a product, especially if it emphasizes new uses. Finally, merchandising is effective in offsetting a move by a competitor, either by holding current customers or by drawing new ones away from the competition.

As part of an advertising campaign, merchandising is directed at three groups: the sales force, the trade, and the consumer. The first task is to be sure that people on the *sales force* are informed about the campaign. Like everything else in advertising and merchandising, this is a matter of communication. Salespeople might be informed through sales meetings in which the campaign is presented; sales manuals, which will help the salespeople do a better job of selling; and sales portfolios to be left with prospects. Companies often add inducements for the sales force, to encourage their support and enthusiasm. Special *commissions* for the duration of the campaign are one way of doing this. Another is a contest for members of the sales force, which often ties in with a contest for consumers.

Trade Promotion

Goals of *trade promotion* are to obtain retailers' support for advertising and merchandising activities, to achieve new distribution, to increase inventories, and to improve relations. Retail support is crucial for the success of other activities. If a special offer is advertised through the media, retailers must have sufficient quantities of the product available and on display. Especially where personal selling is needed—with cameras, for example—their interest and enthusiasm are vital. Merchandising activity also encourages distributors who have never stocked the product to do so. Advertisers always benefit from full store inventories and good relations with the trade.

A number of merchandising devices are used to achieve these objectives. For gaining distribution and increasing inventories, the most common is the *stocking allowance.* The retailer receives an allowance, on either first orders or all orders, for a given time. When the stocking allowance is used to increase the existing inventory of a brand, it is called *loading.* Another form of stocking allowance is *leasing,* in which a company leases part of a store for a short time. Still another variation is the *free goods offer.* The retailer might, for instance, receive one free case for every six sold. To gain cooperation from retail sales personnel, such techniques as special training seminars, contests, and push money *(PM)* are used. PM is a commission for urging ("pushing") consumers to buy the specific brand.

Another group of techniques is employed to encourage retailers' own advertising activity. By mentioning the merchandising effort in their store advertisements, retailers support the larger campaign. An allowance given to the retailer for advertising the product in local media is an advertising allowance. Retailers who arrange their own in-store displays of the product receive a display allowance. POP (point-of-purchase) material is another advertising device. These materials, such as posters and *shelf-talkers,* are sent to the retailer at no charge and with few restrictions. In a typical cooperative advertising agreement, the advertiser and the retailer share local advertising costs equally. Properly used, all of these techniques can benefit both retailer and advertiser.

Consumer promotions have these major goals: to draw new customers, to retain current ones, to load present customers (encourage them to buy a larger supply of the product than usual), to increase use of the product, and to support advertising. The most common forms of consumer promotion are contests and sweepstakes, refunds, samples, premiums, price-offs, and coupons.

Both *contests* and *sweepstakes* offer prizes, usually generous ones. The difference between them is that contests depend on skill, and sweepstakes depend on luck. To win a contest requires the ability to solve a puzzle or finish a sentence about the product, for example. To win a sweepstakes requires luck in having one's name drawn. The disadvantage of both for merchandising purposes is that the contest or sweepstakes itself may draw attention away from the product. An advantage is that they can create excitement about it.

A refund is the return of all or part of the purchase price. Refund offers usually appear in two different places, for two separate purposes. In newspapers and magazines, their purpose is to gain new users. On or in the package, their purpose is to reward present users and instill loyalty to the brand. A relatively new form of refund offer, available in retail stores, is pads of tear-off sheets. In each case, the consumer has to buy the product in order to receive the refund. He then sends the refund offer to the advertiser with a proof of purchase, such as the box top. For the advertiser, an advantage of refunds is that many people buy the product and fail to send for the refund. A disadvantage is that the refund is really a discount, so that the advertiser loses some profit.

Free *samples* seem to work best for new products. They are certainly a strong inducement to try the product at least once. They generally appear as special miniature forms of the regular package. Samples are distributed in several ways: by direct mail, by hand delivery door to door, at retail stores, in shopping malls. In stores, they may be attached to existing packages. For food products in particular, the in-store demonstration has become popular. The demonstrator prepares the product, often talks about it, and offers passersby a taste. All forms of sampling are expensive for the advertiser, but results can be dramatic and well worth the cost.

Premiums are gifts. Those found inside a package, of breakfast cereal, for instance, are in-pack premiums. Their primary advantage for the advertiser is that consumers have to buy the product in order to get the premium. Offering a series of premiums over a longer period of time is a continuity campaign. Near-pack premiums are found in stores near the product. Self-liquidating premiums receive their name because they pay for themselves. A coffee manufacturer might offer a set of mugs imprinted with the company logo, for proof of purchase plus cash. The cash pays for the mugs as well as postage and handling. The mugs are still a bargain to the consumer because the company bought them at bulk wholesale rates. Free premiums are generally attached to the product and are related in some way to its use; free blades packaged with a razor, for example. Premiums of this kind often bear the name of the company or the brand.

The two most common types of *price-offs* are cents-off labels and two-for-one offers. Their appearance is usually confined to a certain production period. For that time, the offer may be printed directly on the label, or on a special sleeve wrapped around the package. Either way, packaging costs temporarily increase. However, there are advantages to price-offs for both consumer and manufacturer. For the consumer, the difference in price is appreciable. Savings are direct and immediate. For the manufacturer, the package becomes an even more effective promotional tool than usual.

A final form of consumer promotion is the *coupon.* Used judiciously, coupons can reduce consumer food bills by as much as 80%. Some sixty billion coupons are distributed in the U.S. annually.

Coupons are distributed by the manufacturer or by the retail store. Manufacturer-distributed coupons can be redeemed at most stores that carry the product; store coupons, only at the store offering them. Like the other forms of consumer promotion, coupons are most effective in inducing trial of a new or improved product. They are also a reward to repeat users. Sometimes a coupon for one product appears on the package of another, related product. This is a *cross-ruff* coupon. A box of pancake mix, for instance, might have a cents-off coupon for pancake syrup. The *self-destruct* coupon is a new form. One coupon is printed partly over another. One might offer a free pack of cigarettes, the other a dollar off on a carton. The consumer has to choose. Therefore, using one destroys the other.

Promotion through minor media

The second broad form of merchandising is promotion through minor media. Anyone who doubts the presence of advertising in a marketing society has only to look around to see that it is indeed everywhere. Any audible or visible means of persuasion, except a person, paid for by advertisers and directed toward consumers, is considered a medium. Scores of minor media exist. The following is an outline of some of the more prominent and effective ones.

1. POP or in-store
   interior display, on-shelf display, public address, checkout counter display, shopping carts
2. outside-of-store
   window display, exterior display, handbills and fliers, wrappings and shopping bags

Time for that fresh-squeezed taste.

Bring home a carton of Minute Maid®
100% pure orange juice from concentrate.
And bring home that fresh-squeezed taste.

3. outdoor
   billboards, sound trucks, posters, aerial advertising, park benches
4. public-gathering
   theater programs and ticket envelopes, trade shows and exhibits, sports stadiums, fairs, hotel lobbies
5. transportation
   car cards in buses and subways, posters in or outside of transit stations and terminals, exterior displays (on buses, for example)
6. directory
   telephone book yellow pages; others, usually specialized by industry
7. direct
   direct mail, mail order, hand delivery to the door (not by mail), telephone
8. film
   for the trade, commercial
9. specialty—most commonly, calendars, pens, and matches
10. newspaper supplements and inserts

Discussion

1. Distinguish between advertising in major media and sales promotion. What is the meaning of "sales promotion"? Give a synonym for it.

2. How does sales promotion relate to brands?

3. What is the relationship between merchandising and advertising? What are the two main forms of merchandising?

4. How can merchandising be effective for a product at both the beginning and the end of its life cycle?

5. What can merchandising not do?

6. What can it do best?

7. Name the three groups toward whom merchandising is directed.

8. Who are the sales force? List several means of sales promotion to them.

9. Who are the trade? Why is their support of the campaign necessary? Name at least three goals of trade promotion.

10. What are some inducements given by companies to the sales force?

11. Explain the stocking allowance. How does it work? What are its purposes?

12. Describe these forms of stocking allowance: loading, leasing, and free goods offer. Do you think these are legitimate sales techniques?

13. What are some methods for gaining the support of retail salespeople?

14. What is the difference between an advertising allowance and a display allowance? Who receives them? Why are companies willing to give them?

15. How else is retailers' advertising activity encouraged?

16. Name several goals of consumer promotion. Name the most common forms of it.

17. How are contests and sweepstakes the same? How are they different? Give an advantage and a disadvantage of both.

18. In what two places do refund offers appear? What is the purpose of each? Name an advantage and a disadvantage of refunds for the advertiser.

19. When do free samples work best? How are they distributed? What is an in-store demonstration?

20. Describe these kinds of premium: in-pack, near-pack, self-liquidating, and free. Give an example of each that you have seen. What is their principal advantage for the advertiser? What is a continuity campaign?

21. What is the major disadvantage of price-offs for the advertiser? What are advantages for consumers and for advertisers?

22. How can judicious use of coupons reduce food bills so much? (In the United States, supermarkets often have double coupon days or weeks.)

23. Who distributes coupons? Who redeems them? What are cross-ruff and self-destruct coupons? What is the purpose of each?

24. Define medium. Go through the list of minor media and consider

the meaning of each. How many are used in your country? What examples can you find? Where?

25. Add to the list of minor media.

Review

Mark T (True) or F (False) for each statement, according to the information in the text.

_____ 1. Advertising supplements merchandising.

_____ 2. Merchandising and sales promotion are synonyms.

_____ 3. Sales promotion can change nonacceptance of a product to acceptance, and build brand loyalty.

_____ 4. What merchandising does best is induce consumers to try a product.

_____ 5. A commission is one form of sales promotion to the sales force.

_____ 6. Trade promotion is promotion to retailers.

_____ 7. When a stocking allowance is used to increase existing inventories, it is called loading.

_____ 8. PM is a form of commission.

_____ 9. The display allowance is a kind of advertising allowance.

_____ 10. Techniques to encourage retailers' advertising can benefit both retailers and advertisers.

_____ 11. Contests depend on luck; sweepstakes on skill.

_____ 12. In order to receive a refund, a consumer has to buy the product.

_____ 13. For advertisers, a disadvantage of refunds is that they are actually discounts.

_____ 14. Samples are free to consumers.

_____ 15. Self-liquidating premiums are expensive for the advertiser.

_____ 16. Cents-off labels and two-for-one offers are examples of price-offs.

_____ 17. Couponing is a big industry in the United States.

_____ 18. A cross-ruff coupon is printed over another, so that using one destroys the other.

_____ 19. POP merchandising takes place inside a store.

_____ 20. Billboards are found outdoors.

Careers in Advertising

Special Terms

Full-service advertising agency
> An agency that handles a wide range of advertising and merchandising services, often all but personal selling.

Account service
> The link or liaison between agency and client.

Client
> The company, organization, or individual that buys the services of an advertising agency.

Communications research
> Evaluation of advertising effectiveness before and after a campaign.

Creative department
> The advertising agency department that oversees all work on copy and illustrations.

Copywriter
> A person who writes the words for print advertising and broadcast commercials.

Layout
> The form showing planned placement of elements in a finished advertisement.

Portfolio
> A representative sampling of a writer's or artist's best work; usually must be presented at a job interview.

Storyboard
> Layout for television. It sketches the sequence of events in a commercial.

Mechanicals
Boards, prepared by artists, on which appear copy, illustration and detailed directions for producing ads.
Typecaster
A specialist in sizes and styles of typography.
Production department
The agency department responsible for the mechanical execution of creative work.
Proofs
Printed from engravings, or metal plates, they are shown to copywriters or proofreaders for checking art and copy before final printing.
Props
Properties. Objects used in a television commercial.
Setting
Where a television commercial takes place.
Traffic department
The agency department responsible for coordinating work among other departments.
Closing date
The deadline for submitting finished advertising to the media.

Vocabulary Practice

1. What is a *full-service advertising agency?*

2. Between whom is the *account service* a link?

3. What is a *client?*

4. What is the purpose of *communications research?*

5. Which work does the *creative department* supervise?

6. What does a *copywriter* do?

7. What does a *layout* show?

8. What is a layout for television called? What does it show?

9. What is a *portfolio?* When is it needed?

10. What are *mechanicals?* Who prepares them?

11. What does a *typecaster* specialize in?

12. Which work does the *production department* supervise?

13. What are *proofs?*

14. Of what word is *prop* the short form? What is a prop?

15. Define *setting.*

16. For what is the *traffic department* responsible?

17. What is a *closing date?*

Careers in Advertising

People in the advertising field frequently warn others not to enter it, although they themselves stay in it. Their ambivalent attitude reflects the excitement, the frustration, the satisfaction, the difficulties, and the rewards of work in advertising. The work causes such contradictory reactions partly because it brings together people of contrasting temperaments and points of view. The world of advertising is inhabited by two groups who are often natural enemies: artists and business people. Artists tend to accuse business people of being dull, unimaginative, and materialistic, concerned only with business. Business people tend to accuse artists of being impractical dreamers, concerned only with creating. The fact is that each group has a great deal to learn from the other. In advertising, as in life, the two depend on each other.

Most people in the field would probably give this advice: "Don't go into advertising if you're afraid of conflict, competition, deadlines, and hard work. Furthermore, don't 'go into advertising.' Decide which aspect of it you're best prepared for, in temperament, interest, and experience. There are all kinds of jobs in advertising. Find the one that suits you best."

This unit describes some of those jobs. It is organized according to the framework of a *full-service advertising agency.* This framework comprises the major job possibilities in advertising and merchandising. It gives an overview of the advertising field and thus provides a final summarization of this book.

The full-service agency began a hundred years ago. Agents, or space brokers, bought print space from publishers in bulk and sold it to individual retailers. Gradually, in order to satisfy customers and to help their own growth, they added other services. As competition increased, they added still more. Today's advertising agency will arrange for its clients virtually every aspect of promotion except personal selling. The typical full-service agency has these departments: account service, research, creative, production, media, and traffic.

How to check out a hot advertising agency.

First let's understand each other.
You want great advertising. You want spectacular sales results from it. You want to like the people you'll work with. And you have no time to waste.

We want clients with guts and imagination. We want mutual respect and we like to have fun. And we don't waste time either.

We want to show you what happens when what you want and what we want come together. We're ready to visit you with three campaigns. All have produced spectacular sales results.

1. Conn Save Yes, SDR does that work. Conn Save's objective was to generate 32,000 home energy audit requests by September, 1981. We did it by March. How we did it will fascinate you. It wasn't just ads.

2. Darien Sport Shop We started in September last year. Fourth quarter sales for this major retailer zoomed up 35% while other retailers were dying. And we didn't spend more dollars either. Just did smarter advertising.

3. Amalgamated Bank of New York They came to Fairfield because they wanted a freshness they couldn't seem to find in New York. They wanted awareness and growth. Our Stiller & Meara commercials helped push this bank over the billion dollar mark for the first time in its history.

**Here's the deal. Call me. I'm Denny Davidoff and I run this agency.
Ask me to show you how we solved any or all of these problems.
You'll get to see what we're like and how we think.
You'll see what makes a hot agency hot.**

SHAILER DAVIDOFF ROGERS Inc.
Advertising, Marketing, Public Relations
(203) 255-3425
Heritage Square
Fairfield, Connecticut 06430
Member American Association of Advertising Agencies

Account Service

Account service, or account management, is the link between the client and the agency. Account managers therefore have responsibilities to both. They work closely with clients to find out their needs and interpret them to the people in the agency working on the account. They carry information and instructions from the client to the various departments. They work with agency personnel to develop plans and suggestions, then take them to the client for approval. Account executives have to be diplomats and good leaders—well organized, ambitious, and decisive. Becoming an account executive is usually a long climb up the ladder, starting from account service trainee.

Research

The job of the research department is to gather marketing data and provide them to other departments. Researchers study and analyze the general market situation and, specifically, the position of competitors. They estimate current marketing potential and forecast future demand. Through questionnaires, surveys, and interviews, they study consumers' values, attitudes, and opinions. A primary purpose of research is to isolate the product benefit, which will trigger the basic idea for the ad campaign. Researchers analyze the product by itself and in comparison to other brands. They compute the likely psychological and financial results of a price or a change in price; the effectiveness of packaging; consumers' feelings about the client company and brand. Media research indicates which media will be most efficient in cost and delivery. *Communications research* evaluates the effectiveness of advertising, both before and after it is used, through tests that measure brand recognition, awareness, and recall. Not all of this will be done at the agency. The client company may have its own research and development department, or the work may be given to an outside commercial research group.

Researchers should be cooperative, well organized, analytical, observant, and intellectually curious. A background in mathematics and statistics, sociology, or psychology—or, better yet, a combination of these—is helpful. Entry-level jobs are as research trainee or research assistant.

Creative

The *creative department* generally comprises the art staff and copy staff. Although "business people" may not like to think so, the creative staff is the center of the agency's entire operation, and is central to the advertising campaign. They are the hub of the agency wheel, and the voice of the client that speaks to the public. Everyone else in the agency supports their work. The creative services department is responsible for all print advertising and broadcast commercials, and often for package design and merchandising materials as well.

Copywriters generally have specific accounts to work on. For print advertising, they write headlines, subheads, and body copy. For broadcast advertising, they write copy, or scripts. Copywriters and artists must be compatible, because they have to work together closely. It is not at all unusual for an artist to contribute copy ideas, or for a copywriter to make suggestions for visuals. Copywriters may even prepare rough visual *layouts* for an advertisement or for a television storyboard. Of course the most important attributes of a copywriter are the ability to use words well and the desire to use them for commercial purposes. Copywriters should be able to write concisely and with flair, to communicate clearly, and to work with others. They also need to be resilient; they may be asked to redo again and again work that they thought was brilliant the first time. Since they are most successful when they can put themselves in the place of consumers, empathy is another useful characteristic. For a potential copywriter, a background in advertising, literature, psychology, sociology, philosophy, or languages is helpful. Job seekers are usually required to show a *portfolio,* a collection of their best work. Entry-level positions are as copy cub or junior copywriter.

It might seem that an artist should have a way with drawing, just as a copywriter should have a way with words. This is not necessarily true anymore. Today's advertising artist, or art director, is expected to create concepts, not finished art. In a large agency, rough sketches are enough. There are two reasons for this. To the work of the agency, the concept is most important. Everyone is able to work from that. In addition, a large agency usually contracts out finished work. The agency hires art buyers who deal with photographers, art studios, and freelance artists as necessary. Nevertheless, the artist is ultimately responsible for all visuals: for an advertisement, the design or layout and the illustrations. For television, the layout is a *storyboard,* which illustrates the sequence of action in a commercial. Artists also prepare *mechanicals,* boards with type, art, and detailed directions for producing advertisements. They may be responsible for specifying type size and style; or specialists called *typecasters* may do this. Although drawing may not be part of a job, it is a skill usually necessary to get the job. Like copywriters, artists should have portfolios of their best work. Talent, imagination, and ability to communicate clearly are desirable characteristics of an artist.

Production

Production may be part of the creative department. There is an increasing tendency to unite the two, since they must work so closely together. Production is responsible for the mechanical execution of the creative work. The production staff supervises the manufacture of

P&G Up Against Its Wall
Feb. 23, 1981

advertising, both words and pictures, for all print media. The work itself is given to outside suppliers who take a mechanical, shoot it with a camera, and make an engraving, or metal plate. From the engraving, they print *proofs.* Proofs are given to copywriters or proofreaders for checking. Final proofs are shown to clients for approval. Print production specialists work with artists and copywriters, advising them about the characteristics of various graphic art techniques.

Broadcast producers used to handle radio and television programming. Now networks, independent producers, and local stations do. As a result, the major responsibility of today's broadcast producers is to supervise production of commercials. Television producers prepare budgets and select directors, camera people, musicians, and other technicians. They locate independent production studios. They work with copywriters and artists to transfer storyboard to film or videotape, or oversee live commercials. They supervise casting of actors and selection of *props* (properties, all objects used in the commercial) and *settings* (where the commercial takes place). Radio producers work with writers and often with musical directors and sound effects people. Being a broadcast producer requires a rare combination of skills: business, artistic, and diplomatic. The usual entry-level job is that of broadcast production assistant. Any kind of training or experience in a film or tape studio, or with a radio or television station, is very helpful.

Media

The job of the media department is to choose the media for the client. This means having all available information about the media, analyzing it, planning the media mix, making recommendations to the agency and the client, and contracting with the media. The essence of the job is to deliver the right package to the client: a plan for how and where to reach the appropriate audience, in the most cost-efficient manner. Fortunately, in a large agency the media director doesn't work alone. Media planners organize data and write plans. Media buyers negotiate purchases of space or time with publishers or broadcasters. Media estimators make charts that show purchases, dates, and costs. In a small agency, all of these jobs will be combined. Media people should be thorough, dependable, organized, and able to negotiate. Previous work in media research or sales is excellent background, as is a degree in marketing, economics, statistics, or business administration.

Traffic

The traffic department keeps everything moving. It is responsible for the coordination of all activities. The traffic department handles all necessary approvals. Traffic people move from one department to another, making sure that everyone is working harmoniously and on schedule. They see that *closing dates,* deadlines for sending advertise-

The Fisher-Price Mama Bear and Baby Bear invite bear hugs.

Our motherly mom and her baby bear are a couple of honeys.

Mom, in printed blue smock and ruffly white cap can be dressed and undressed, even by your youngest child. And look at her sweet face. You just know she's thinking how much she loves her baby bear.

You can imagine how much fun it is to have these velvety-soft, easygoing bears around.

They don't mind getting knocked about. They love to splash in washing machines and romp in spin dryers because they're totally washable.

And they're absolutely unfazed by the idea that little toddler humans are handing out the bear hugs for a change.

ments and commercials to the media, are met. If the creative department is the hub of the agency wheel, the traffic department is the lubricant. No particular background is necessary, but accumulated knowledge of all agency workings is imperative.

In a small advertising agency, positions are not so narrowly classified, and one person will have a greater variety of duties. There are even one-person agencies. For any job in advertising, the best broad experience is gained through working in a retail store, in any capacity. Retailing gives the ambitious, observant, enthusiastic, and interested person constant opportunities to see how consumers behave and how products work.

Discussion

1. Why do many people in advertising have an ambivalent attitude toward it?

2. What do "artists" and "business people" often say about each other?

3. Why would anyone say "Don't 'go into advertising'"?

4. How did the full-service advertising agency come about?

5. Name the departments of the typical large agency.

6. What is the function of account service? How do account managers carry it out?

7. What are desirable characteristics for account managers? How do they often begin?

8. What is the job of the research department in general? Describe specific duties of researchers in these areas: market, consumer, product, media, and communications research. Who besides the agency might do research?

9. Name desirable qualities for researchers. What kinds of background are useful? What are entry-level positions?

10. Why are the creative people "the hub of the agency wheel"? What are their general responsibilities?

11. What do copywriters do? Why must they be compatible with artists?

12. Describe the characteristics of an ideal copywriter.

13. Why is it often not necessary for artists to draw finished work?

14. What are the general responsibilities of artists? What other specific responsibilities might they have?

15. Give reasons for combining the creative and production departments.

16. What is the production department responsible for? Who often does the actual finished work?

17. Explain proofs. What are they? How are they made? How are they used?

18. What did broadcast producers do in the past? Who does that work now? What is the major responsibility of broadcast producers now?

19. Name the specific duties of agency television producers.

20. What do agency radio producers do?

21. What skills should a broadcast producer have? How do people in this job usually start out?

22. Briefly, what is the major job of the media department? Specifically, what does this mean?

23. In a large agency, media work may be divided among media planners, buyers, and estimators. What are their respective tasks?

24. Describe the nature and duties of the traffic department.

25. Why is work in retail stores the best preparation for work in advertising?

Review

Fill in the blanks with appropriate words from the text.

1. The world of advertising is inhabited by ＿＿＿＿＿＿＿＿ and business people.

2. An agency that handles a wide range of advertising and merchandising services is a ＿＿＿＿＿＿＿＿ agency.

3. The company, organization, or individual that uses an agency is a ＿＿＿＿＿＿＿＿.

4. Account service is the link between the _____ and the _____.

5. Market researchers analyze the general market situation and, specifically, the position of _____.

6. They estimate current market potential and _____ future demand.

7. _____ _____ evaluates the effectiveness of advertising both before and after it is used.

8. The creative department generally comprises _____ and _____.

9. The person who writes the words of a commercial is a _____.

10. A layout for a television commercial is a _____.

11. It is no longer necessary for artists to draw on the job. Rough sketches are enough because the _____ is more important.

12. Artists prepare _____, detailed directions for producing advertisements.

13. To get jobs, artists need _____ of their best work.

14. The _____ department is responsible for mechanical execution of creative work.

15. _____ are printed from engravings, checked, and approved before final printing.

16. _____ are objects used in television commercials.

17. Where the commercial takes place is the _____.

18. The _____ department in an agency keeps everything moving.

19. Closing dates are _____ for sending advertisements and commercials to the media.

20. The best preparation for work in advertising is any job in a _____ _____.

Index of Special Terms